A SHORT PRIMER
FOR
UNSETTLED LAYMEN

HANS URS VON BALTHASAR

A Short Primer
for
Unsettled Laymen

Translated by
Michael Waldstein

With a Foreword by
Angela Franks, Ph.D.

IGNATIUS PRESS   SAN FRANCISCO

Title of the German original: *Kleine Fibel für verunsicherte Laien*
© 1989 Johannes Verlag, Einsiedeln

Cover calligraphy by Victoria Hoke Lane

Cover design by Roxanne Mei Lum

First English edition © 1985 by Ignatius Press, San Francisco
Printed with ecclesiastical approval
Foreword © 2020 by Ignatius Press, San Francisco
All rights reserved
ISBN 978-1-62164-434-7 (PB)
ISBN 978-1-64229-126-1 (eBook)
Library of Congress Control Number 2020938406
Printed in the United States of America ∞

CONTENTS

FOREWORD

What does it mean to be "unsettled laymen" (*verun-sicherte Laien*)? More precisely: What does it mean to be unsettled laymen today?

The Church herself is unsettling, of course, a "sign of contradiction", as Simeon said of the infant Jesus (Lk 2:34; cf. Acts 28:22). The Church is unsettling because she is the nexus wherein the infinite God unites himself spousally with fallen yet redeemed man. "This is a great mystery, and I mean in reference to Christ and the Church" (Eph 5:32).

Here, however, Hans Urs von Balthasar's use of *verunsicherte Laien* does not refer to the disconcerting awareness that the Church, as the Body of Christ, will not bend to suit passing fads and fallen desires. This unnerving feature of Catholicism is treated by Balthasar in other works.

In this *Primer*, Balthasar addresses today's faithful laity who feel that precisely this solidity of the Church is shifting beneath their feet. He speaks to those who fear that the Church has done what she ought not to do: that she is in fact relaxing her demands in order to win favor, not from God, but from man.

But has she not always done so? Balthasar is much too historically informed to think that today's condition of *Unsicherheit* (uncertainty, unsettledness) is unique to our age.[1] Indeed, what about the Church has always unsettled the faithful laity? Is the problem not the complicity of those within her, even at the highest levels, with the world, the flesh, and the devil?

Nevertheless, there is something new to what unsettles the faithful laity *today*. Man has always made pacts with the contemporary spirit of his world. Today, when Christians accommodate themselves to the world, they are accommodating themselves to a modern reality that *by its very nature attempts to unsettle and uproot*. This fact makes the contemporary *Unsicherheit* even more disorienting.

Modern thought and imagination valorize the self-made individual. Elsewhere, Balthasar calls this "the Prometheus principle", an evocation of the titan Prometheus' misguided attempt to overthrow the divine hierarchy through providing the technology of fire to human beings.[2] This "titanism" emphasizes man's freedom and his creative ability. He can use his freedom to shape the world and himself. Indeed, he must do so.

---

[1] See his treatment in "Casta Meretrix", trans. John Saward, in *Explorations in Theology*, vol. 2, *Spouse of the Word* (San Francisco: Ignatius Press, 1991), 193–288.

[2] See Hans Urs von Balthasar, *Theo-Drama*, vol. 2, *The Dramatis Personae: Man in God*, trans. Graham Harrison (San Francisco: Ignatius Press, 1990), 417–24.

What is good in this world view is captured by the era of the Catholic Baroque. Take Gian Lorenzo Bernini's statue of Saint Teresa in ecstasy. Surrounding the scene of her intimate experience of divine love are spectators, who sit in theater boxes erected on the walls of the side chapel: the Cornaro family, which commissioned the art. They do not just watch; they gesture, converse, and pray.

The Christian art of the Baroque has a lively sense of the theo-drama of salvation history, a drama in which we cannot remain mere spectators. As free persons, we must either consent or refuse to play our creative role in the drama of God's infinite and free love encountering the sinful world.

The Christian balance expressed in Bernini's art depends upon the insight that the Christian can create only because he is first created. In other words, God's creative activity in forming human nature and persons has priority—it sets the terms and the boundaries—before any subsequent creative activity.

But atheistic modernity rebels against this prior receptivity and opts for a technological *creatio ex nihilo*. This is secularization: the rejection of a transcendent origin and goal for man. The infinite horizons of man are closed in around him. Atheism "is the postulate that man ... must not owe his existence to anybody except himself".[3]

While this immanentizing of man's horizons was supposed to liberate him, this apotheosis instead

[3] See below, 136.

deeply disoriented him. Now he was supposed to create himself out of whole cloth. He need not consult his nature, a category that is rejected because it interferes with the imperious enactment of the will on what must become passive matter. Increasingly, man cannot consult his ancestors, because these have become only a barrier to his freedom, and maybe they are even themselves constructed, as in the case of designer babies and donated gametes. Further, communal and cultural ties are increasingly relativized or liquidated.

This is the modern loss of "form" (*Gestalt*), a loss of meaning and structure that Balthasar mourns in his multi-volume *Glory of the Lord*. Practically speaking, it means that institutions and people often seem to be making things up as they go, trying on now this identity, now that, like clothes off a rack. Yesterday's politically correct language is forbidden today. Yesterday's mission statement must be revised today as the institution reinvents itself.

This insecure situation marks the Church in distinctively new ways because it is doubly unsettling. First, when Christians surrender to the world today, they surrender to the unrealizable demand of self-creation. This leaves them deeply disoriented. Second, the faithful laity encounter this insecurity not only in their own spirit but also in Catholic institutions and persons, as these, too, accommodate themselves to the liquid spirit of the age. Everything seems to be shot through with instability.

Into this situation Balthasar re-proposes the "form" of Jesus Christ as revealed in his Church. This form is "only the whole": the whole, concrete reality of Christ, conveyed within Catholic tradition.[4] This form is "spun from three strands" of Word, sacrament, and ecclesial authority.[5] These three provide the Church with the ability to remain on course despite the winds blowing through history.

This triply woven tapestry was triply threatened in modernity. The Enlightenment constricted *logos* (word, reason) to the bounds of human reason alone. This ruled out the possibility of revelation, in which the transcendent *Logos* speaks to man. "Through the 'demythologizing' examination of Scripture, the figure [form again!] of Jesus fell apart."[6] Further, "progressivism" emerges. But it ironically consists of a regression, as it moves away from the divine mystery—*sacramentum* in Latin translates the Greek *mysterion*—to a shrunken anthropocentrism.[7] Lastly, "liberalism" asserts man's freedom as ultimate authority, which requires a rejection of Church authority.[8] In this way, the three strands constituting the whole tapestry of Christianity unravel from within, whenever these modern mind-sets color theology and ecclesial life.

---

[4] See below, 35.
[5] See below, 39.
[6] See below, 42.
[7] See below, 46–48.
[8] See below, 49–51.

Against this diminution of Christianity, Balthasar holds up "the center, the whole" of the form of Christianity, seen especially in the saints. Mother Teresa, for example, "embodies [it] effortlessly", in particular because there is "nothing ... progressive, nothing traditionalist" about her.[9] The form of Christ is not a matter of picking sides.

In fact, Christianity opts for the "Catholic 'and' ", as Balthasar calls it elsewhere.[10] This is the Catholic tendency to say "both ... and": both nature and grace, both God and man, both one divine nature and three Persons. This does not mean that any idea or practice that claims to be Catholic is genuine and must be absorbed into Catholic life. Rather, it means that the form of Christ is, as Balthasar said, "only the whole".

"Only": as a form, it has a definite shape and is not just an amorphous reality that could be anything at all. We read the Bible, not other sacred books. We worship in a liturgy with a structure that seems unyielding. This form makes demands on us. It is not negotiable.

But also "the whole": this form is as wide as the infinite God. It is not a limit on thought and freedom but their healing. This "whole" is summarized in the Creed.[11] The form of Christ as

[9] See below, 25.

[10] Hans Urs von Balthasar, *The Office of Peter and the Structure of the Church*, trans. Andrée Emery (San Francisco: Ignatius Press, 2007), 329.

[11] Exegeted in von Balthasar's text below, 83–88.

expressed in the Church includes the "catholicity" (the universality) of the Church, which is lived out in a variety of states of life and ecclesial forms. Central among these is the form of Mary, who "*is* the Church that gives her assent, and everyone in the Church has a part in this assent".[12] The "Petrine" office of Church authority exists to support the Marian *fiat* of every Christian.[13]

This *fiat* is made possible by the Cross of Christ, "the way by which God brings about reconciliation".[14] The Cross unites the "horizontal" hope for this world with the "vertical" impetus of mysticism. But it also provides "the third thing, which alone leads to the breakthrough, the great suffering that is like the synthesis of action and contemplation".[15] In the Cross, "pain and death receive meaning" and are "revalued": they now become the means, not of self-dissolution, but of union with God in eternal life.[16] "Whoever would save his life will lose it . . ." (Mt 16:25).

"Only the whole" of the crucified God-man both distills and swells the otherwise fluid horizons of man. "The only thing that brings salvation is concentration upon the one form that is at the same time unequivocal and eucharistically all-embracing,

[12] See below, 101.
[13] See below, and 110–18.
[14] See below, 94.
[15] See below, 33–34.
[16] See below, 91, 93.

the only one that is wide open to the infinite, to triune divine love, and just as open to creation."[17] This form is beautiful, good, and true, and it is the origin and goal of all created beauty, goodness, and truth. In this form, we find the security that grounds and opens up our freedom to the infinite.

Angela Franks, Ph.D.
Professor of Theology
St. John's Seminary
Easter Monday 2020

[17] See below, 138–139.

PREFACE

This is a primer in which the children of God will find initially unfamiliar written signs for the sounds of faith with which they are familiar, signs that are intended to correspond to these sounds. By laymen, we mean above all Catholic laymen.

The Lord advises Christians to remain simple in love, like children, for God revealed his mystery only to the simple, while the wise and clever (Jesus thanks him for this) do not grasp anything of that mystery. Children believe the stories they are told. They would be astonished, they would not even understand, if they were told that what they hear and repeat is a "science" and that the stories need not necessarily be true. The illiterate in the faith is usually more sure and unbiased than the literate, who always runs the danger of burdening others with the letter and pinning them down with it. "Knowledge puffs up, but love builds up" (1 Cor 8:1). What is puffed up is hollow; what is built up remains.

But the unfortunate thing is that, with their supposed science, the wise and clever, often enough theologians, unsettle the simple. The latter feel in their correct instinct of faith that something is fishy, but they do not find the correct answer. This is why Jesus speaks the frightening words about the millstone that is to be hung around the neck of the tempter of one of these little ones; this is why he threatens the "scribes and Pharisees" who lock the doors to the kingdom of heaven, do not enter themselves, and deny the entrance to those who want to go in (Mt 23:13). They think themselves superior to the simple Christians but are not even able to distinguish anymore between worldly exercise of power (*kyrieuein*: Lk 22:25) and the spiritual authority (*exousia*: Mk 3:15) granted by Jesus to his disciples and those who take their place, an authority over the spirit that is against God, an authority to bind and loose on earth with effect in heaven. In being so scientific, they have become unable to believe in the Trinity or Christ's divinity or his real presence in the Eucharist. Such things appear to them a "party jargon" (we are quoting); and that, dear Christian parents, is what they are teaching your children in the schools today.

Therefore, the people who are unsettled, despite their good instinct, need to have a short primer placed in their hands so that they may find for their inner vision of Christian truth at least an outline of a few written signs that they can show to their tempters. Yet those whose "eye is sound" and who are therefore "full of light" (Mt 6:22) should not disturb themselves by imagining "that the scientific theologian knows 'more' about the truths of faith than an upright Christian who seeks to live those truths day by day or that a biblical scholar understands Scripture 'better' than a simple monk who has been meditating on it for years" (P. Henrici).[1] Nobody should suppose that he ought to embark on lengthy studies that he will scarcely be able to finish, in order to emerge at the other end of the dark tunnel into the daylight of simple faith or—a great danger—to get stuck in inflating half-knowledge. This primer may suffice as a first orientation.

Not everything that disturbs the unsettled will be dealt with but only the most urgent questions concerning the faith and its situation today. Questions on Christian morals cannot be clarified in such limited space because insight into the binding character of a moral norm depends largely upon how deeply a Christian has penetrated into the understanding of his faith. The fullness of faith in its unity must be experienced anew.

This little book addresses unsettled laymen. Is it too audacious to hope that some of those who have done the unsettling will also pick it up and let themselves be unsettled here and there in their settled self-confidence?

[1] "Die Aufgabe Kirchlicher Wissenschaft Heute", *Philosophie und Theologie* 54 (1979): 326.

THE SITUATION

All true Catholic Christians suffer today from the confusion within their Church. One can safely say that this unrest that followed the council came mainly *from the clergy and religious*. By leaving their state of life in large numbers and by the secularization of the theology, catechesis, and preaching that they practiced, they proved that they thoroughly misunderstood the "opening of the Church to the world" intended by the council. Laymen, living and engaged in the world, did not need to feel addressed by this slogan as much. The increased apostolic commitment in the political, economic, and social spheres that was demanded was nothing fundamentally new for them. But the shock to the clerical world could not remain without influence on the lay world. This influence became all the more confusing as perfectly normal conciliar reforms, such as that of the liturgy, were mixed up—inextricably, for the laity—with innovations in statements of faith, catechesis, preaching, and ecclesial practice that were most unworthy of belief and that the laity quickly recognized as unecclesial. These disorders were justified as legitimate by their authors in many ways and were cemented theoretically and practically, so that calls to order by higher authorities, if they came, generally died away without any effect.

This situation was made more severe by the massive appearance of a sort of "intermediate state" in the Church: the state of the (male) *lay theologians*. Without doubt, there were true laymen among them who wanted to give a better foundation to their service to the Church. But there were certainly just as many who would in earlier times have decided to become priests and who for this reason often enough harbored resentments against the clerical state and propagated its sociological and, as far as possible, theological secularization. A line of demarcation divides this state. Of course the state of lay theologians is powerful only in some countries, while in others it exists scarcely or not at all. In any case, the new phenomenon is a strong support for the trend toward blurring or completely abolishing the boundaries between the clerical state and the "worldly" lay state. The worker-priests, from different motives, had already pressed toward at least a temporary synthesis of the two forms of life. Now many clerics claim that they are undergoing an identity crisis and that they can no longer determine their place in modern society. Marriage appeared a place of refuge, all the more because it seemed that the increasing lack of priests could be eased by "proven" husbands and because women began to strive for the priesthood on the basis of their equality with men. Has not much of this been successfully practiced for a long time by the communities that split off from the Catholic Church? One can see that these are all clerical problems. One cannot say that the growing number of lay theologians has become the mouthpiece for the true concerns of the laity, which has been present in the Church since the beginning.

In some of its reforms, the council lightened certain burdens. For example, it abolished mandatory abstinence on Friday, limited fasting, and also simplified the liturgy. But this lightening of burdens was fused with a completely different "lightening" pushed through by the secularized clergy (always including a large number of religious) in the practical sphere (for example, the sacrament of confession was almost completely lost) and especially in the sphere of faith, where a small or large question mark was placed behind almost every article of the Creed. This fusion led to *two grievous sociological-ecclesial facts*.

The first fact was the quiet exodus of innumerable Catholics from church on Sunday, where an alien doctrine, no longer bearable to Catholic ears, was often proclaimed from the pulpit. This exodus often ended with a complete turning away from the Church.

The second fact was the spectacular secession of different more or less radical groups of traditionalists, who either openly denied the legitimacy of the last council or regretted some of its regulations or loudly protested its effects. Supported by individual bishops, they oriented themselves completely to the preconciliar period by wishing to preserve the entire Creed but walling it into the letter of a liturgical form that was no longer recognized.

Both of these tendencies led a great number of laymen to distance themselves from the life of the Church, alienated by the spectacular identity crisis of clerics or religious, which was often quite unnecessarily talked about from the pulpit. Those who behaved so theatrically before them did not in any case correspond to the image of a priest [*Geistlichen*], someone who has been seized and illumined by the Spirit [*Geist*] of God, someone to whom a layman can turn and upon whom he can rely as a leader on the way to God. For the layman, the priest is still the man who gives visible expression to the hidden nature of the Church and to the demands made by Christ in the Gospel, the man who according to Paul is a *typos*, a pattern by which one can orient oneself. Therefore it was and is easy for the layman to distinguish, among the priests he knows, between those who deserve the name and those whose failure he perceives, whom he perhaps patiently endures or, if they are worse, by whom he is scandalized. From the point of view of the layman, there is no possible change in the identity of the priest. Thus their identity crisis is an occasion for him either to look for his "spiritual leaders" in a different place, for example among the masters of Eastern meditation, or to stick to the proven preconciliar wine while letting stand the must that behaves so absurdly, until perhaps it has cleared up somewhat.

What has been said so far seems to lay the blame for the present crisis one-sidedly on only one state within the Church and to exonerate the other completely. Justice demands a supplement. The world is engaged in such rapid movement that change has become for the man of today a kind of constituent part of his experience and view of the world. What refuses in principle to change appears suspect. Can a religion that has for two thousand years professed the same Creed without change and demanded it of its members, a creed in which central historical facts occur, still be credible today? This faith is so old that it seems it can "scarcely still be true". Many parts of the Christian world (not all) are permeated by a *secret weariness* of articles of faith and forms of devotion that are always the same. Something more in tune with the times should be found or, if need be, invented. Feuerbach and Nietzsche (the son of a pastor) were laymen. Laymen in the Church are also gripped by this yearning for a completely different way to the Absolute, for a voyage to new shores such as Nietzsche hoped for.

But perhaps this leads us back to the earlier perspective. In the first centuries of the Christian era, the absolute newness of the message of Christ was something fascinating. In the history of the Church, this inner, essential, and unsurpassable newness was experienced and lived out before the world again and again, especially by the saints. (Just think of Saint Francis of Assisi.) Is not the manner in which the revelation of Christ was proclaimed in modern times (on the basis of an arid Scholasticism that had become rationalistic), and also perhaps the absence in many lands of great saints, a reason why this faith seems outdated? Were some attempts at making Christian life more timely too artificial, too external—for example, the attempt of "Catholic Action"? Was that smouldering yearning for something completely different and authentic already so strong under the rigid traditional education of priests in seminaries, novitiates, and scholasticates that the fertile suggestions of reform made by the council were not seriously considered but immediately overrun and used as a pretext for trampling down that of which one had long since secretly become weary?

However that may be, the present situation is characterized by a strong *polarization* in the Church, so much so that a dialogue between "progressives" and "traditionalists" succeeds only rarely. The camp of the progressives seeks to conquer the center; that of the traditionalists holds the fortress tenaciously as if it defended the center. Both sides distance themselves from the men in office and the small number of theologians who seek to maintain the true center.

Where should one look to see a dawn? One should look to where in the tradition of the Church something truly spiritual appears, where Christianity does not seem a laboriously repeated doctrine but a breathtaking adventure. Why is all the world suddenly looking at the wrinkled but radiant face of the Albanian woman in Calcutta? What she is doing is not new for Christians. Las Casas and Peter Claver did something similar. But suddenly the volcano that was believed extinguished has begun to spit fire again. And nothing in this old woman is progressive, nothing traditionalist. She embodies effortlessly the center, the whole.

The upcoming generation is understandably highly suspicious of the image that the Church presents by and large. Thus it easily becomes the prey of the magic of youth religions that demand some wild and often absurd commitment. Yet there are some who want to make their way back through the undergrowth to the true sources of Christianity. They are waiting for help. The greatest and *most difficult task of the contemporary Church* lies here. A great number of the radiant preconciliar figures of theology, spirituality, and pastoral care have disappeared. The generation in between, formed by the storms and confusions after the council, dominates the theological landscape, holding the teaching posts, pulpits, and positions of leadership. Can the young people who are seeking what is authentic be led by this generation that dominates the present (or by bypassing it?) to what they dream of? It depends upon the success of this leading whether Christians tomorrow will regain spiritual leaders whom they recognize as giving back authenticity to them and to the whole Church. The vigilance and especially the prayer of everyone are required.

The short primer presented here cannot anticipate the future. Its purpose is merely to offer a few guidelines for the present. It is not a catechism that justifies and explains the individual aspects of the Christian faith and shows them in their context, much less a worked-out theology or even the outlines of one. It offers merely a few signposts at crossroads where one could take the wrong path, merely a compass that indicates where north is in each case. The compass has the advantage that it need only point and not prove. The primer has the disadvantage that it cannot prove in sufficient detail many things to which it points. But the premise of the primer is that the light of Christ to which it points proves itself and thus repels what is false; it is *index sui et falsi*. Thus everything depends upon whether the light of Christ in its incomparable unity becomes evident.

THE INCOMPARABLE

To know humanity is to know that *religion* belongs to its essence; it is to understand how the different forms of the one world religion were born from the human yearning for the Absolute. Man is generated: he does not produce himself. However strong his sense of clan may be, he knows that he owes his being, not merely to his parents, but, with them and all ancestors together, to a generative first cause. Although he is very distant from this first cause because of transitoriness and because of the guilt in which the whole fabric of the world is entangled, he must nevertheless bear a certain kinship to it. Thus he can imagine the Absolute as a personal being, as a multitude of such beings, or (because of its sublimity) as superpersonal and impersonal. From the images and symbols with which he is familiar, he can and must form myths of the beginning, maintaining, and perishing of the world and think himself, the mortal, into an encounter with the imperishable and into a judgment of the dead with reward and punishment. Perhaps (who knows?) everything begins anew after the completion of an age. But perhaps, if an especially enlightened teacher shows the way and method, one can escape the continuous flow of perishable rebirths and find one's way back into the first cause from which one fell, alienated, into the finite. At the same time, since man is a social being, there is a public-social religion of the state in which a ruler represents the cosmic order, the divine principle that dwells in the world. The religions of the temple and of the court are in this case organically interwoven. "Wise men" and "prophets" as officials of the commonwealth can interpret and translate the laws and ordinances of the totality of nature into the practical-moral and practical-political sphere.

With the *Hebrews* something fundamentally new and awry breaks into this religious world, even though they appropriated many (transformed) elements from it. The present moment, the establishing of a covenant between a man (Abraham), indeed a people (on Sinai), and the Godhead is for them only the firming of a *promise* that points to the future and end of human history. Although the people are now nomadic, now wandering through the desert, now languishing in temporary or final exile, a yearning for the promised messianic kingdom burns ever more intensely in them. God gives "instruction" (law) for the way through the times that must be endorsed by faithfulness to the Covenant, an instruction that is at times actualized by prophets but that is not, as long as the fulfillment is lacking, "written into the heart". It therefore has a

certain external character ("tablets of stone"). When
it is absolutized "for religious motives", it can lead
to a terrible confusion of the law and the God of
the Covenant who decrees it freely ("Pharisaism").
Inasmuch as God, who chooses and promises, breaks
into history with sovereign freedom, the world and
mankind appear as his gratuitous creation, radically
demythologized. Thus late Judaism, tired of waiting, could lose patience and wish to bring about the
messianic kingdom by its own power, to make its
way to it through history in dialectical rationalism
or in utopian hope.

On the foundation of Judaism, the *"third generation"*, the *Christians*, rises as something completely
new, indeed, as the conclusively new reality that at
the same time integrates what is valid in paganism
and Judaism. This new reality rests on the incomparable claim of the man Jesus of Nazareth to be
able to speak and act with the authority of the God
of Israel and the Creator of the world, the claim
to be the conclusively valid Word of God to Israel
and the whole world, as a human being and not as
a hero or demigod as the pagan religions imagined
him. This unsurpassable claim, which also demands
an unconditional "following", is presented with
incomparable humility, naturalness, and closeness
to the poor and despised and also always as a fulfillment and yet unexpected surpassing of Old Testament prophecy. Because this fulfillment did not

correspond to the earthly-eschatological aspirations of the Jews, Jesus was rejected as a false messiah and crucified by the Roman authorities. But through his Resurrection, he was confirmed by God as the true Promised One and beyond that as God's final self-manifestation and self-giving to the world. What is manifest fulfillment in the Risen One remains an "earnest" for Christians, and thus it is hope in a much more concrete and comprehensive sense than in the Old Covenant. The distance from the Jewish hope becomes clearer still if one considers the gesture, meaningless for a human being who does not participate interiorly in the divine life, of distributing himself, his death that is suffered for "us all", in advance as food and drink for the disciples then and for all followers from then on. The final event did not merely happen, to be proposed as an ideal for all generations; it is given and completely surrendered in order that it may continue to be proclaimed and distributed in the Holy Spirit of this God who gives himself eternally.

Nothing remains of the timeless *mythos* of the world religions except the human symbols from which it was constructed. The core of Christianity is simply history. God not only spoke into this history but embodied himself in a human destiny. The outlook to the end of history is lifted into a completely new hope: the hope for the salvation of mankind and the cosmos as a whole on the basis of God's free entering into all the darkness of the world's destiny. This is incomparable as an offer and a chance. If one falls out of it, one sinks back into Jewish messianisms and pagan paths of flight from the world.

WHY STILL CHRISTIANITY

There is much talk today of the necessity of opening new means of access to the understanding of
Christianity. The apologetics that was successful in
earlier times, it is said, is hopelessly outdated. Often
the oldest apologetics, the one closest to the original
phenomenon of Jesus Christ, is also the newest and
most effective. Should not the whole timeliness of
Christianity today be visible in the elementary fact
that *it alone* in the history of the world is *the superior
unity of paganism and Judaism*, then as today?

Even in her earliest days, the greatest difficulty of
the Church was to bring together the religious tradition of Judaism and its expectation of the Messiah
with the pagan forms of piety that seek in different
ways a present contact with the Deity without religious hope for the future. The issue today is still
the same synthesis, and it has become more pressing
than it was then through the products of secularized Judaism. (Only this secularized form is meant
here; there is certainly still a believing Judaism.)
What has to be brought together today is the justified concern for the future of mankind, which has
more than ever been entrusted to human capacity

and responsibility, and the inalienable demand that every individual think here and now of his relation to God and his eternal salvation. Man must give himself completely in two directions: *the horizontal "forward"* and *the vertical "upward"*. And this should be accomplished in such a way that each direction does not hinder the other but, on the contrary, furthers it.

But how is this possible? How could a person such as the Marxist, who is absorbed completely in the service of future mankind's well-being, have the time and desire to pray and to collect himself in God? On the other hand, how could someone who practices Eastern meditation and submerges himself in the Absolute dedicate himself completely to his earthly task?

The vertical and the horizontal cross only in the Cross of Christ: only in him is the dedication to mankind perfectly one with the immediate contact with the Father's will. Why? Because the will of God for which Christ listens in prayer sends him always anew into the world and its distress, not with merely human programs, but with a plan of salvation that can be thought and realized only by God. Action alone is not enough; even in Jesus' life on earth it did not reach its goal. Prayer is not enough; it points at first always to action but finally to the third thing, which alone leads to the breakthrough, the great suffering that is like the synthesis of action and contemplation: the bearing of the unbearable guilt of the world that had barred the access to God forward as well as upward. The door is now open in both directions.

Forward: What good are the Marxist plans for the future if humanity cannot be essentially changed and if the innumerable past generations remain unredeemed? The Christian works for change in the world in the hope, initiated by Christ, of his return, the hope of the coming of the kingdom of God that will transform everything and integrate into itself every effort for the good.

Upward: What good are all the ecstasies and submersions practiced in Eastern techniques if they do not encounter the living Heart of God, the absolute love that proved itself in the Cross of Christ, a love with which we never become identical but that gives us a share in itself in the Holy Spirit?

Man remains stretched between heaven and earth without ever bringing the two dimensions of his existence to a final harmony by his own power. Does this not show that from his creation he has been designed for the Crucified and Risen One in whom his restless heart finds rest?

The same point can be expressed even more simply with the Gospel: the two main commandments, the love of God and the love of neighbor, become one only in the One who is at the same time God and man. This incomparable fact is and remains the center of Christian apologetics.

ONLY THE WHOLE

It remains incomparable only if the figure of Jesus Christ is not cut to pieces. Cunning pretexts are invented for breaking away various parts from this figure here and there. But the more fragmentary and supposedly plausible the figure becomes, the more unintelligible it becomes in reality.

One aspect always points to all the others, just as in an orchestra the playing of a single instrument becomes meaningful only in harmony with all the others. An example: if Jesus *is* God's Word made man, then he not only *speaks* marvelous things but also *does* them. And among those deeds, the spiritual deeds are greater and more marvelous than the material: forgiving sins, as he himself says, has precedence over bodily healing. But even these signs that he performs on the blind, the lame, and the possessed are revelations of divine grace in human form; anyone who denies them robs the Incarnation of one of its aspects. Another example: How could Jesus demand of his disciples an unconditional following, even a daily carrying of the cross, if he did not know that he was to go this way first and as the paradigm for all? His demand would become

unintelligible if one denied him this awareness. A
third example: in his behavior one finds often contrary features: the greatest tenderness can combine
with extreme abruptness. But if one keeps before
one's eyes that he is really the Word of *God* in
human form and that in God what is seemingly
most opposed is one—omnipotence with highest patience, judgment with mercy—then it is not
possible or necessary to smooth out and level what
is seemingly irreconcilable in the behavior of Jesus
according to the standards of an average psychol-
ogy. The fire that he "came to cast upon the earth"
can very well be at the same time fire of wrath and
fire of love.

These are only examples of the inner coherence
of the figure. One could and should continue at
length to show the proportions of this figure of the
Savior Jesus. They can be compared to the well-
balanced statics of a Gothic cathedral. But these
statics remain unendangered only if one leaves
complete the faith of the primitive Church as it is
expressed in the writings of the New Testament.
It is quite natural that this faith can approach the
figure of Jesus from very many and even contrary
sides that complement each other in their forms of
expression, corresponding to the infinite relations
of meaning present in the figure; it is quite natural
that there is not just one but that there are four
Gospels, each of which has its own point of view.
How could God's Word, even God's incarnate

Word, who lives and suffers, dies and rises, be caught in the dungeon of a few human words? "The world itself could not contain the books that would be written" (Jn 21:25). But the accounts circle around the central mystery in such a way that, for the one who wants to see what is being shown, it makes a convincing impression and the faith demanded of him seems meaningful. This faith, like the faith of the first disciples, is always a response to God's Word.

The faith that expresses itself in the New Testament is not the faith of isolated individuals but that of a community. This community is linked to its founder; Jesus had himself chosen, trained, and commissioned its nucleus, the Twelve. As a community, it knows that it is entrusted with continuing his concerns and even his presence. Therefore, this communitarian faith remains normative for all who want to join the community. And to believe, since it includes following, never means merely theoretical assent (dogmatics) but, just as immediately, means a practical rule of life (ethics) that is also normative for the individual since it is an expression of the lived community of faith. The old Church called this *disciplina*.

Even at an early point, people who stood outside (Gnostics, Ebionites) began to contest the figure of Jesus. But the faith of the community watches over the figure's integrity, and the faith of the individual remains sound by joining itself to the faith of the community as it takes shape in the writings of the New Testament and keeps itself alive in the communal realization of the Lord's memorial, the Eucharist.

SPUN FROM THREE STRANDS

Besides the word that is proclaimed and the sacrament that is celebrated, a third aspect, already hinted at, is needed to tie the Church to her origin with a cord that is spun from three strands, namely, the authority that had been given from the very beginning to the chosen Twelve as a participation in the authority of Jesus (Mk 3:14f.). In the time surrounding the Passion—at the institution of the Eucharist ("Do this in remembrance of me": Lk 22:19) and after the Resurrection ("Receive the Holy Spirit. If you forgive the sins of any ...": Jn 20:22f.)—this authority is deepened to become priestly power. From Peter's first appearance in the Acts of the Apostles, through the strict Church regime exercised by Paul in his communities, to the teaching of the First Letter of Peter about the task and attitude of the "shepherds", it is clear that the Church is structured by office, even though, under the apostles' eyes, the precise structures took shape only gradually.

In order to see *the interpenetration of these three aspects*, one merely has to observe that the office is known and understood just as strictly in the

commission and service of Christ as Scripture
testifies to this commission (in accordance with
Christ's own attitude of service) and as the central sacraments—the Eucharist and absolution from
sin that separates from the Church—are depicted
as entrusted to the office. Only in the commission
of Christ can a man meaningfully say the words,
"This is *my* Body" and "*I* absolve you". The office
must thus itself be a sacrament received from Christ
or those commissioned by him. Nobody can claim
such authority on his own, not even the community as such; authority, as Scripture attests, can be
possessed, administered, and passed on only as a gift.
*Scripture, office, and sacrament all point beyond them-
selves* to their institution by the original and permanent giver, Jesus Christ, who himself exercised his
authority and power only in humble service to the
Father's will.

All three stand in the service of the spiritual
enlivening of the community in which the Word
of Scripture should be lived and responded to
(Scripture, of course, always contains the believing
response of Israel and the Church), the community
in which the activity of the office should engen-
der in all believers an activity in proper responsibility, the community in which sacrament and
liturgy should be the leaven of the whole everyday
life of Christians. The *objective holiness* that dwells
in Scripture, sacrament, and office has the purpose of fertilizing the *subjective loving holiness* of the

members of the Church. For this subjective holiness is the one that, according to the will of Jesus, is to convince the world of the truth he brought. That which is printed, institutional, and liturgically performed remains sterile if the seeds that lie in it do not sprout, fertilized by grace, in the field of hearts.

Scripture, office, and sacrament belong to the inner being of the Church but are instituted by the Lord. Her tradition, filled with tensions throughout history but always drawn into unity, guarantees the Church of Christ her identity. The life of the tradition proves itself not only by engendering a credible following of Christ ("holiness") through the centuries but also by the fact that in times of spiritual trouble, the office, supported by theology's contemplation and research, protects by definitions the central content of the Christian faith against aberrant curtailments and brings out anew the entirety of the figure of revelation. Aspects of the mystery that have so far remained in shadow can also be brought into the light in agreement with indications of Scripture and the liturgical tradition. But they may not change the basic proportions of the nature and action of Christ.

ENLIGHTENMENT

This unity of revelation and historical tradition, and thus the insight into the whole, was called into question only in modern times. It was questioned for the first time in the Reformation, which tore the principle of the office from the fabric we described by deriving this principle, not directly from Christ, but from the community, thus endangering the fullness of the sacramental aspect. At least the "*I* absolve you" spoken in the name of Christ became impossible; but the "This is *my* Body" also became problematic.

The decisive operation occurred in the Enlightenment. In great part, the Enlightenment was certainly brought about by the quarreling among Christians. Behind the "denominations", people sought a position that could neutralize the opposition of denominations by attempting to reduce them to the level of criteria that can stand their ground before human reason. The correlation of the figure of Christ and the faith of the Church (borne by Scripture–office–sacrament) was broken off. Through the "demythologizing" examination of Scripture, the figure of Jesus fell apart.

Inconsistencies, for example, in the accounts of the Resurrection led to doubt in the attested facts, including the Resurrection itself. The miracles could have been invented or at least strongly exaggerated. The sayings of Jesus may have been stylized and elevated to a greater authority than he himself claimed. The infancy narrative may have been added from legends. The meaning of his death on the Cross and its assessment by Christ himself is uncertain. Similarly uncertain is the exact significance of his words and gestures at the Last Supper. Through such questioning of the texts (contrary to their clear intention—but the text is "conditioned by the times", the enlightener knows better), the figure of Jesus pales to that of the founder of a religion, comparable to other founders. His incomparable uniqueness that cannot be mastered by reason disappears. He becomes a perhaps significant moral paradigm in a "religion within the bounds of unaided reason".

Of course, together with the dissolving of the figure of Christ as it had been known in faith up to this point, the interpenetration of Scripture, office, and sacrament is also removed. Just as Scripture becomes a text of the history of religion that can be questioned "critically" in a neutral scientific manner, so also the office attested in it loses its christologically based authority. It appears sociologically as a function within a certain religious community, quite comparable to analogous functions of other religious communities, most of which also have their offices and "priestly ranks". The same holds for the sacramental liturgies, for which there is much that is comparable in other religions.

When one summons the correlation of the claim of Jesus and the faith of the Church before the tribunal of "unaided reason", even just as an experiment, and when one brackets faith with even just a "methodical doubt", then the neutral space that opens is immediately occupied by the demand for a "free discussion" about the meaning and import of the truths of faith.[1] In this way, for example, the divinity of Christ, although it has been defined quite solemnly by general councils, can be put up for discussion, whereby naturally the mystery of the Trinity of God, that of the Church, that of the sacraments, and many other mysteries become questionable at the same time.

The principle that was always held up to this point by ecclesial theology that the article of faith embraced in a living faith must be the basis and point

[1] "Elementary conditions of the realization of faith are called into question if even the appearance is given that one cannot talk freely about questions of faith.... Faith stands and falls with the right of the individual Christian to communicate to others his personal understanding of the message proclaimed by the Church and to speak to them in all openness about it.... The Church can only remain alive as a community of faith and love if everybody can express his opinions, problems, and questions without immediately having to fear suspicions, words of rebuke, and the prohibition of discussion or even the allegation of dishonest motives." *Stimmen der Zeit* (1979), 793.

of departure for a deepened rational reflection—just as the attempt to understand a work of art better must always proceed from its entirety—this principle is no longer valid. One should rather *step behind faith*—its act as well as its object—*in order to gain from this point the decisive light on faith.*

PROGRESSIVISM

The paradox of what is called "progressivism" in the course of the realization of the Enlightenment has hereby become evident. For it consists in a *regression* behind the correlation of the contents and the act of faith. Thus the enlightened exegete goes back behind the accounts of miracles in the Gospels in order to show from the sphere of common stories of miracles of that time that Jesus' miracles are "nothing special" but rather a part of that "general phenomenon" that reason can explain in this way or that. Or he inquires behind the redaction of the Gospels for their sources in which (perhaps) the faith of original Christianity is expressed in a much more primitive and undifferentiated form or where a view of the world becomes evident that could not be followed by those who came later and was therefore covered up by them. As a theologian, he gives the name "late theologies" to the fully developed forms of theology in the New Testament that seem to give too much weight to certain simple facts, and he seeks his way back to the traces of earlier stages that are closer to simple human understanding and do not require such a *sacrificium intellectus* as does, for example, the Pauline faith in the nature and effect of the Cross of Jesus.

Once the chief assertions of Scripture are summoned before the judgment seat of unaided reason, their interpretations by the Church must of necessity be subjected to the same procedure, no matter how solemn the authority is in which these interpretations are vested. For they have not joined in the decisive regression behind the article of faith and remain therefore uncritical and naïve for the enlightened spirit.

Some have *attempted to mediate* between the standpoint of the faith of the Church and that of the Enlightenment by setting up the principle that each theological assertion, i.e., each assertion that concerns God, must also be an anthropological assertion, an assertion that concerns man, not accidentally, but in his essence. In one respect, this principle is of course correct. For not only does God reveal himself to give his gifts to man, to free him from his entangled situation, and lift him to participation in the divine life, but man must also be able to understand somehow—in the self-abandonment of faith—what is intended for him and to draw the moral consequences from it. Yet the principle mentioned is deeply ambiguous, and this unreflected ambiguity is an innermost characteristic of the situation in the Church after the Enlightenment. For it can also be interpreted in the sense that each assertion about

God must be tried and approved before the tribunal of human reason. The most extreme form of this demand is present in Hegel, for whom there is no mystery in God that is beyond human understanding once God has disclosed himself fully. Few who wish to be counted as Christian theologians go as far, but many stress the second part of the principle so strongly that the greatest possible general intelligibility of a revealed truth is made into the principle of its interpretation. The attempted step beyond the mystery is necessarily the dividing of a whole that cannot be seen through in its unity, for example, the unity of divinity and humanity in Christ. The progressive position always presents itself as the attempt to dissolve a historical "amalgam" for the sake of easier understanding. But John warns: "Any one who goes ahead [*pās ho pro-agōn*] and does not abide in the doctrine of Christ does not have God" (2 Jn 9) because he "dissolves Christ [*lyei Christon*]" (cf. 1 Jn 4:3).

LIBERALISM

The situation that arose with the penetration of the Enlightenment into theology is something thoroughly new for the Catholic Church. The touches of Catholic Enlightenment in the eighteenth century dissipated soon, while the Protestant and increasingly also the Anglican churches were plagued by it as by a serious disease. I remember a conversation with Karl Barth that took place in the 1940s, in which he said with a sigh: "You Catholics have it good; at least you know what you have to keep to in matters of faith. We others have to get along with people whose supposed faith is miles away from what we consider evangelical truth." Barth saw clearly, of course, that *this tragic situation is due to the absence of a binding teaching office.* He attempted to keep all the more closely to the Word of Scripture and used to stress that everybody who loses his way by going behind the Word necessarily finds himself in darkness, a darkness that deepens the farther he goes. In virtue of this principle, he was able to give living witness in his splintered church—a witness, however, that lacked the means to counter the division effectively.

He overlooked or did not wish to notice that the original synthesis in which the believer knows and acknowledges the fullness of truth includes an authoritative ecclesial teaching office that is released by this synthesis into time. The office simply must proclaim, and preserve for the sake of proclamation, the indivisible truth in its organic coherence. Therefore every theological interpreter of revelation must always orient himself by this norm to which the living office points, both together with and in regard to Scripture.

Since these conversations with Barth, theological liberalism has also penetrated deeply into the Catholic Church. One realizes this best in the open and ever more vehement contesting of the Magisterium's rights concerning doctrine, while the contesting of the truths of revelation is usually camouflaged diplomatically. This game of hide and seek with seemingly "orthodox" formulations in which a liberal (i.e., enlightened rationalist) meaning is hidden is a new phenomenon and highly confusing to the layman. Confronted with single assertions of a theologian, the decision whether one is dealing with a truly faithful or a liberal assertion can become almost impossible. It becomes a different matter only when one takes into account all of his assertions and his whole attitude toward the Church. But even here, the decision whether a theologian is "Christian" can be very difficult, especially outside the Catholic Church. Think of Rudolf Bultmann, who was without doubt deeply pious and closely linked to his Christian origins. In the case of Catholics, the diagnosis is easier because of the inner bond between Christ and the Church, his Word and sacrament, and their steward, the ecclesial office. But even here, the difficulty can be increased by the inflation within the theological sciences of "neutral" subjects that one can pursue equally well as a believing Christian or as an unbeliever: for example, the comparative science of religion or studies of Eastern language and culture with their interdependence. Liberal theology finds an optimal hideout behind the anthropocentrism of these subjects.

Another very effective hideout of liberal-rationalist theologizing—the demand for the reinterpretation, by councils or even by Scripture itself, of old formulations of the faith that are supposedly or really no longer (easily) intelligible—will be dealt with soon.

PLURALISM

Scarcely any catchword that has spread into the Church from the circles of theologians has had more success than "pluralism". It has always been self-evident to the Church that the divine mystery cannot be reduced to a single conceptual formula. For this reason, the Church has always known and sanctioned a plurality of theological forms of expression. But the talk of pluralism is a new phenomenon in her history, as new as the establishment of a liberal theology in her midst.

The Bible itself is plural in its external and internal construction. All kinds of literary genres stand next to each other: narratives, laws, visions, poems, and letters all circle around the mystery of God who discloses himself in the world. The four different Gospels, each with its own point of view and its own theology, show very clearly that the incarnate Word of God will not let himself be imprisoned in a deadening letter. Throughout the history of the Church, different schools with their particular perspectives on the mystery confronted each other. How could and should it be otherwise? The one blinding light is broken by a prism into many colors, which surround it in a circle and can therefore confront each other in contrasting fashion.

Contrasting, but *not contradictory*. Plural, but not pluralistic. For the word pluralism has been invented specifically to make even contradictions between theological opinions legitimate. For one theologian, Christ is the Son of God, one in being with the Father; for the other, he is not. There may be quite different words and concepts by which the Gospels grope toward the mystery of Christ, but everybody will understand that the opinion of the New Testament about Christ cannot be contradictory in itself. We can go farther and say that, however the first communities may have been organized structurally, some this way and others that way, it cannot have been the will of the apostles, who determined the structure, to plan or even to tolerate contradictory structures: for example, next to a "hierarchic" structure in which chosen heads, approved by the apostles, led the community, a purely "democratic" structure in which the community consecrated its leaders by its own authority and enabled them to perform sacramental acts. Rather, one can definitely say that, even if we cannot reconstruct each step in the train of thought whereby the disciples arrived from an intimation of Jesus' transcendent origin to the insight into his true divinity, even if we are equally unable to observe every phase of the organization of the community under the supervision of the apostles to the point of its independent structuring with a bishop and his body of presbyters, we certainly know enough to be able to imagine this path from the implicit to the explicit without contradiction. Thus, it is not possible to go back today to an "Ebionite" stage of the christological development of the New Testament (a stage in which Christ is practically only a superprophet, as in the Koran) and to construct from this stage a Christology that is possible and legitimate in the Catholic Church today. It is just as impossible to pick up the thread from the hypothetical structure of a community without a "head" (e.g., that in Corinth)[1] in order to make legitimate today a "democratic" Church structure next to the hierarchic structure.

There is no valid reason to speak of a "new" theological pluralism simply because the secular sciences have grown to such an extent that no individual can gain an overview of them. The theological auxiliary

---

[1] Certainly leaders of some sort existed in Corinth. In the Letter to the Philippians, they are expressly mentioned together with deacons, and Paul certainly did not establish two fundamentally different community structures in such close vicinity. These leaders may have been with Paul when the letter was written. Besides, Paul sends his official collaborators to Corinth for an "apostolic visitation". In the *Didache*, which may have already been written in the middle of the first century, "prophets" appear next to permanent officials as leaders of the Eucharistic celebration. This probably happened with the approval of the apostles. The structures are consolidated slowly under their eyes. They are fully developed in the Letter of Clement (circa 96), not only in Ignatius (circa 115).

sciences are spreading out likewise, but they cannot unearth facts that would essentially change the core of the revelation of the Old and New Testaments. This core still remains the same. On the one hand, it is historically fixed in the actual events and documents; on the other hand, it is so overrich in content and at the same time such a provocative scandal for "pure reason" that all generations until the end of the world will be sufficiently occupied with it.

This core is protected from being relativized to the point of theologies that contradict each other by three facts: first, God's Word, not just some word, expressed himself in human form and intelligible speech; secondly, this incarnate Word was sheltered in the written word, not by just any authors, but by authors who were inspired by the divine Spirit; thirdly, an office that was instituted by Christ and is led by his Spirit watches that the essential doctrine remains pure. What is sealed threefold in this way is *an authority "above theology"* to which every theology in the Church must orient itself and by which it can be measured in its truth content. Justified and needed plurality always has a point of reference above itself by which it must orient itself. This guarantees the unity of theological reflections among themselves and prevents their disintegration into pluralism.

EXEGESIS

Closely connected to the plurality of biblical ways of access to the mystery of revelation stands the contribution made by exegesis to its understanding. Since, taken abstractly in itself, it is a neutral philological science, it can be practiced by a believing or an unbelieving scholar, but of course in a very different spirit. Jesus demands a radical Yes or No to his person and claim. What is "neither hot nor cold" is spat out. Someone who wants to "bracket" this claim "methodically", even if he does so only provisionally, in order to wait and see if this claim was really made and, if so, if it was made rightly, exposes himself to the danger of a neutrality that is forbidden by the object and falsifies it. Certainly there are different stages of assent to Jesus in the Gospels, as his question shows: "Who do the people say that I am? ... But who do you say that I am?" But this holds for the period of his earthly life, when his entire form could not yet be seen as a whole. Once this form was brought to its completion through the Cross, Resurrection, and return to the Father, it can be and demands to be seen and acknowledged in its indissoluble unity. The one who is either unable or unwilling to see it will attempt again and again to dissolve it into disparate parts and thereby invalidate its claim.

A wide field of research is at the disposal of Catholic exegesis, even if it cannot join in such attempted dissolutions. The figure of Jesus arrives at its fullness through his life, death, and Resurrection—only at the end of the "history of its essence" (Schlier) did God's Word become fully man. In the same way, the various approaches toward seeing and understanding him grow together only gradually from many perspectives, just as many brooks unite to become a river that can carry ships. However, whereas in the case of a river one can no longer distinguish the origins of its waters, a comparison of the different versions of texts in the Gospels often allows a return to the preliminary stages in which the entire figure was necessarily still seen imperfectly and partially. One can also show how the different evangelists use their sources in different ways for their total vision. The synthesis does not lie in the texts of the Gospels; these, rather, point beyond themselves to the one incarnate Word of God, Jesus Christ, in whom alone dwells the fullness of all truth.

Thus it is to be expected that in verifiable preliminary stages of the text one finds at times a faith that is not yet formed but still expecting, a situation acknowledged openly by the evangelists when they stress that the disciples did not understand the decisive point at all before the Resurrection.

It is a completely different question whether Jesus'
consciousness of his being and mission was only
in development at first: if, for example, we can
verify a stage of his consciousness in which he proclaimed the coming of the kingdom of God without any connection yet to his person and destiny.
In this case, the evangelists would have projected
Jesus' final self-understanding back into the early
period of his proclamation from the vision of the
whole brought by Easter. But with some reflection, such assertions seem highly improbable. For
Jesus' bearing distinguishes itself from the outset
from that of a mere prophet. The kingdom arrives
with his arrival; blessed the one who is not scandalized by him.

In the building as a whole, as we have already
stressed in the beginning, each stone carries the
whole wall so unequivocally that all the question
marks placed upon it by exegesis cannot shake its
compact structure. That Jesus gave himself in the
Cenacle cannot be called into question by the fact
that the words of institution have come down in different versions, versions that, incidentally, converge,
revealing the inner wealth of the mystery. Likewise,
the Resurrection cannot be called into question
by the fact that its experience by the disciples was
broken into different facets. The divine fullness of
that which offers itself in an incarnate event necessarily goes beyond the limits of a single linguistic
formulation.

The way back from the present text to its preliminary stages leaves room for many hypotheses.
Thus the opinions even of Catholic exegetes may
be diametrically opposed. But they cannot possibly afford a neutral distancing from the faith of the
Church as it is expressed simply in the Creed and in
the liturgy. *For the place in which the decisive confluence
of all individual views about Jesus occurred is the original
Christian faith of the community.* In its womb and for
the sake of its faith and certainly according to its
standard, the whole of New Testament literature
came to be. The plurality of that literature shows
only the wealth of its inner unity. That a certain
aspect could dominate in a certain community or
group did not disturb this unity.

If one keeps this crystallization point of the Christian faith before one's eyes, the point from which
and for which the writings of the New Testament
were composed, then exegesis loses its alarming
aspect that endangers and undermines faith. It will
then be self-evident to the believer that someone
who does not acknowledge this central point and
does not wish to read the texts from it and toward
it can achieve results that dissolve the Christian faith
partly or completely. But the neutrality of science,
including philology, remains preliminary in relation
to this final decision of faith, a decision called for
in face of the whole phenomenon of Christ that
stands, for the one who has eyes to see, without
comparison in the history of the world. In its inner

coherence, this faith cannot possibly be the fabrica-
tion of a few uneducated fishermen who brewed up
a fable about a god-man after Jesus' death.

Exegesis of the New Testament practiced in an
ecclesial spirit can be just as fruitful and illuminat-
ing for the fullness hidden in it as is the *exegesis of
the Old Testament* according to universal opinion.
For more than a century, the latter has enriched our
understanding of the theological depths of Israel's
history in an unexpected fashion. What appeared
earlier as flat and two-dimensional received a hith-
erto unknown three-dimensionality through the
distinction of sources, through chronology (e.g.,
the chronology of parts in a prophetic book such as
Isaiah or Jeremiah), and through the contributions
of archaeology and the comparative history of religions in the Near East. In addition, much has been
clarified in this field in the course of the research
of the last decades. Many points that were exaggerated have been refined, and a general consensus
is in the making despite the divergence between
individual theories.

While the formation of the Old Testament canon
occupied many centuries, New Testament exegesis
is confronted with a few decades—indeed, more
precisely, with only a few years—between the death
of Jesus and the faith of the Church that was suddenly present and complete. Paul receives the hard
core of the Creed even in Jerusalem and Antioch.

And though he unfolds it according to his vision of the exalted Lord, he does so "handfast" with the original apostles, the "pillars" of the Church (Gal 2:9) in whom the memories of the time with Jesus were still alive and fresh. Everything lies very closely together. There is no time for the formation of myths. Without a doubt, the collection of the memories of Jesus, of his Passion, and of his sayings began very early for the edification of the communities and for their liturgies and preaching. The reasons given for the late date of the composition of the Gospels (after the destruction of Jerusalem) may rest largely upon prejudices.[1]

Again, nothing is more normal than that a comprehensive understanding develops through the summary of previous particular visions of the whole. This is all the more true because in Jesus the many disparate lines of Old Testament prophecy intersect. One could interpret his suffering, for example, in the light of the "destiny of the prophet" or of the atoning value of the just man's suffering, or finally, and more exactly, in the light of the servant of God who suffers vicariously. In the Cenacle, the Covenant

---

[1] Cf. M. Hengel, "Christologie und neutestamentliche Chronologie", in *Neues Testament und Geschichte, Festschrift für O. Cullmann* (1972), 43–67, and his essay, "Zur Entstehung der Vorstellung vom stellvertretenden Sühnetod Christi", *Int. Kath. Zeitschrift Communio*, vols. 1 and 2 (1980). Cf. also the book, certainly still to be checked at many points, by J. A. T. Robinson, *Redating the New Testament*, 3rd ed. (London: SCM Press, 1978).

on Sinai, together with the blood poured out there, reaches its fulfillment, as does the Paschal Lamb, the New Covenant promised by Jeremiah, and at the same time the servant of God who is delivered up for the "many". If we leave to the mystery of Jesus its all-fulfilling vastness, then exegesis can help us to realize this fullness more and more deeply.

But one thing will never be possible: namely, that some human science should lift itself above this fullness of God and sit in judgment upon it from above. Today, especially in France, all kinds of "modes of reading" Scripture (*lectures*) are fashionable: a structuralist, a psychoanalytical, a materialist, and finally a historical-critical reading. These attempts contradict the simple basic rule of all science that the object determines the method appropriate to it and that only the method determined in this way can be considered adequate and "scientific". Here the object is Jesus Christ, certainly in human form but with the claim of proclaiming God's final word to the world. No purely worldly method can be the one demanded by this object unless it subordinates itself as a humble instrument to the only appropriate response to the Word: the faith of the Church.

THE FREEDOM OF THEOLOGY

No science can be free in relation to its own object: it becomes a definite discipline next to others only through that object. It is scientific only if its method of research corresponds to the specific nature of the object. The object of theology as a "science" is the Christian faith with all the specific characteristics of its nature. It has an origin in history but claims to reveal in its message at the same time the meaning that embraces history as a whole, its beginning and its end. The lamb of Revelation breaks open the seven seals of the history of the world. Christian faith also has a history essential to it on account of its historical origin: the history of its being witnessed to and lived, which belongs inseparably to the object of theology.

Can a science have a voice in determining its own object? It cannot do so in the sense that through it the object could be changed or called into question, but only in such a way that it is extended further or limited to a special field or that its relations with other adjacent fields of research are investigated. In this way also, a theologian can deal with the whole content and act of Christian faith or with only a part of it. For example, he can deal with the faith that is expressed in the writings of Paul, together with a consideration of its connections to the contemporaneous Jewish faith and the Hellenistic forms of religion. But changing its object is something theology cannot do. Its scientific freedom lies in the choice of the appropriate points of view and methods by which it intends to illumine its object from within.

An example will clarify these abstract assertions. In the Gospel one finds the assertions: " 'I am the resurrection and the life; he who believes in me, though he die, yet shall he live.... Do you believe this?' [Martha] said to him, 'Yes, Lord; I believe that you are the Christ, the Son of God, he who is coming into the world' " (Jn 11:25–27). What positions can be taken on these words? What freedom does theology have here?

1. One could say that these words express the view of an individual or a group of believers toward the end of the first century whose faith objectified itself in these words.

2. One could say further that the formulation is the end product of a faith in a historical event but that these words preserve a "superimposed interpretation" conditioned by the times.

3. One could hold the view that these words were spoken as they are written down.

4. Finally, one could think that these words are the summary, correct expression for a historical

event as the faith of the original Church understood and interpreted it.

Is Christian theology free to join one of these four opinions? If its object is the original Christian faith as it was understood in its nature and handed down through the centuries, then it cannot join the first opinion because Christian faith intends to refer to the historical event of Jesus Christ, his life, death, and Resurrection, and in fact loses its object without this reference.

But Christian theology will not be free seriously to hold the second view, either, since the alleged "superimposed interpretation" expresses not only the common faith of the first formed communities but also the faith formulated in the official Creed of the Church, in her liturgy, and in the personal witness to faith by Christians through the centuries. This faith is the object of theology, and one cannot reach behind it by questioning. It is possible, as has been said, to bring to light the way in which this faith reached its full unfolding from preliminary stages and implicit forms and formulas, a process that is to be expected from the nature of things.

The third "biblicist" or "fundamentalist" view can be held, but it has to face the "historical-critical method", which for its part in Christian theology cannot question the inner content of the faith but only its outer formulations.

With regard to the fourth view, many critical questions are possible. If they are to remain questions of Christian theology within the "scientific" character proper to it, they will move within the interrelation of the fully formed Christian faith, as the whole of the New Testament writings express it in many ways, and the object of this faith, as the same writings attest to it. This object leaves freedom for an inexhaustible number of perspectives, synchronic and diachronic. One can oppose the different points of view of the authors and gain thereby a stereoscopic picture. One can, as was said, seek to observe approximately the development of the fully formed formulas. It is possible that in this process certain modes of behavior displayed by Jesus, the incarnate Word of God, the Word that thus speaks through his entire humanity, were subsequently put into concentrated linguistic words that—having come to be under the direction of the divine Spirit—contain at least the essentials of what Jesus expressed.

In this research, of course, all boundaries of Christianity with contemporaneous Judaism and paganism can be considered, too; vocabulary and imagery can run across the cultures and religions as common property. But the history of theology clearly teaches that such excursions into spiritually neighboring countries always lead to a return to the homeland. The things borrowed are fewer than one thinks, or they are at the same time so much adaptations and reinterpretations that what is specific to Christianity clearly outweighs what seems to be held in common. There are numerous influences of all great and small adjacent cultures upon Israel, reaching into very intimate and central areas. And yet, every time this has been established, that which is incomparably Hebrew emerges again more clearly. It is impossible that Jewish and Hellenistic influences should be lacking in the New Testament, but for the most part they do not shape the images of Jesus; rather, his image, towering over everything and not to be compared with anything, imprints itself on the different cultural spheres.

So much on the freedom of theology within its object: the interrelation of the Word of God and the faith of the Church. One cannot, however, ignore the fact that in the understanding of this object two views stand opposed to each other. According to one view, the continuity between the object (centrally Jesus Christ in his life but also in his death and Resurrection) and the faith of the Church is brought about by the office instituted by Christ, the choice of the Twelve, their being furnished with authority that they exercised decisively in the apostolic Church and handed on to followers. In the other view, this official authority of the apostles who founded and ordered the Church is absorbed in the only remaining authority, that of Scripture. The Catholic Church and the

Orthodox Church stand on the one side; the Protestant communities stand on the other.

The consequences of this disagreement for the
understanding of the freedom of Christian theology
are considerable. If there is no ecclesial office that
derives its authority from Christ, then there exists
no normative continuity between the faith of the
original Church and the faith of the Church today.
Only the Word of Scripture remains as a norm.
Although this Word describes the interrelation of
the original Christian faith and its object, it is not
evident why historical-critical questioning should
not be able to reach behind it in this witness. If this
happens, a completely new form of freedom enters
the historical science that deals with the Bible.
Depending upon the depth of the penetration, this
science will have little more than the name in common with a theology that knows an apostolic official tradition. The two forms cannot be combined.
For in the first form of theology, an authority is
present that binds one to the essential Creed in harmony with the witness of Scripture. In the second
form, where *sola scriptura* has validity, the question
remains whether Scripture alone can bind one to
such a creed. Some will answer this question in the
affirmative: Scripture has enough strength in itself
to attest to itself as the unsurpassable Word of God
and to make its claim prevail. Others will answer
in the negative, since Scripture as a historical doc-
ument can be brought before the judgment seat of

the reason of today that evaluates what is historical in a new and different way.

It is astonishing to see Catholic theologians, who should hold on to a living tradition that is theologically relevant in virtue of the apostolic office, pleading for a freedom of theology that consists in thinking that theology's object, the faith of the original Church attested by Scripture, may be abandoned or reinterpreted in its essential assertions. This faith is, of course, a binding of oneself to a truth recognized as unsurpassable, the New and Eternal Covenant in Jesus Christ's perfect surrender of himself, through which man receives a new and abundant freedom. It is a freedom "bought" for him through this surrender of the Son of God unto the most godforsaken death, the highest possible price. It is a freedom that gives to the believer a participation in God's own Spirit, in which, according to Paul, he can judge everything while being judged by no one (1 Cor 2:15): certainly the most superlative thing that can be promised and given to a human being. Is it possible that somebody would wish to exchange this Christian freedom that unfolds within the covenant of love with God for the watered-down, tasteless freedom to question precisely this most precious gift?

DOGMA AND LIFE

A parenthetical remark at this point: while liberal
ideas in the drafts of Catholic theologians about
dogma conceal themselves mostly under orthodox formulations, they dare to emerge much more
openly where the issue is the practice of Christian
life. Nor can one deny that little or nothing can
be drawn from the letter of Scripture regarding
the application of general rules of conduct, for example, the sexual rules: contraception, abortion,
the way the Church deals with remarried people or
homosexuals. For this reason, the individual ethical ordinances of the Church are today considered
arbitrary and thus largely changeable, if not alto-
gether superfluous. And since this appears evident
to many, a feeling of relativism and legitimate pluralism penetrates into the sphere of dogma from the
sphere of practice. Indeed, the frequently discussed
ethical questions of conduct tend to be placed at the
center as the decisive problems of mankind, while
the questions of dogma are pushed to the side, prin-
cipally because of their alleged uncertainty.

But Christian revelation is in the first place God's
self-manifestation and self-giving to man in Jesus

Christ and in the Holy Spirit. The miracle of this living and loving gift of God certainly demands a human response, a word of thanks that is not merely spoken with the lips but witnessed to by life. But God's Word is the first thing; the human response is second and, moreover, is oriented completely according to the form of the first. One can see this easily from the structure of Paul's Letters. He speaks first of the mystery of God in Christ; then the consequences for Christian life are drawn from it. Their particulars are determined and chosen according to the situation of the community and are therefore necessarily incomplete. But what is important is the bond that ties all moral rules of conduct to the archetype, Christ. This bond is strong enough that a valid inference can be drawn even for questions of life that are not expressly mentioned in the Epistles or the Gospels.

Not without reason does the example of Paul play such an important role in the mediation between dogmatic truth and the life of the community. The apostle, by being completely expropriated of himself and living only for his ministry, is the embodiment of the Church of the saints who follow the footsteps of the Lord as closely as possible and can thereby serve as a mediating and concretizing example for the other believers who are also in principle saints by virtue of their baptism. "Be imitators of me, as I am of Christ" (1 Cor 11:1). And because Paul knows that he is so completely under the spell of Christ's all-surpassing love, he can say in one place, "I wish that all were as I myself am" (1 Cor 7:7). He alludes to his virginity in these words. But he immediately adds corresponding rules of conduct for married people.

This shows that what is first of all clear is the dogmatic truth about the person and achievement of Christ and that one must proceed from it, and thus "from above", to deduce from this truth the rules of Christian life. It shows, secondly, that the perfection of Christian discipleship is set up within the Church as the first standard for Christian life. This perfection can be lived in very different ways according to the spiritual gift given to each person, but it consists essentially in selfless, crucified love (1 Cor 13). It can demand much of man, because everything was demanded of the Son on the Cross. The ethical instruction of the Church must therefore begin from above and then see how far it can go in making concessions "downward" to human frailty. It must not attempt to be more "merciful" in this respect than God in Christ. Above all, it must not build up Christian behavior from the lower limit of what can barely still be permitted and leave the striving for holiness to a few outsiders as exceptional and peculiar behavior.

When the Church thus thinks from above downward in moral questions and gives corresponding instructions, she simply follows the movement of revelation and the style of the apostolic Letters.

The first concern is the most fitting response of
the believers to God's surrender to the point of the
Cross, a response that must come from the gratitude and joy of the new life with the Risen One.
Both things are true: "[Let] him deny himself and
take up his cross daily" (Lk 9:23) and "My yoke is
easy, and my burden is light" (Mt 11:30). Gratitude
shows itself in the generous will to surrender that is
exercised in one's daily dealings with one's neighbor (the love of neighbor is the sum of the law and,
beyond that, "my commandment", the "new commandment") but also in the instructions for married
life and family life and for behavior during the liturgy and elsewhere in the community.

REINTERPRETING

Only now can the other catchword, the "reinterpretation" of biblical and dogmatic assertions as well
as of instructions of the Church demanded today,
be meaningfully dealt with. Nobody should let
himself be confused by the incomprehensible and
frequently hollow theological jargon about "herme-
neutics" that often serves only to camouflage dan-
gerous shifts in the assertions of faith. Three things
must be distinguished:

The words of Scripture. Since they are filled with
the Holy Spirit, they are always new in themselves
and should be read anew, pondered anew, and in
this sense reinterpreted by each individual. But they
stand on a foundation of rock, while the world
changes all around them: "Heaven and earth will
pass away, but my words will not pass away" (Mk
13:31), *stat verbum dum volvitur orbis.* For this reason, each interpreter must remain in the ranks of
interpreters that go past the Word and hand down
to each other the meaning they found. *He will
seek the meaning that is shown to him today in no
other place than in union with the Church.* For only
the Church is at once both the immediacy of the

presence of Christ and his Word (in sacrament, in office, and in lived faith) *and* identity through history and through the succeeding generations, who are all our brothers and fellow believers in Christ and in the Holy Spirit. It would be profoundly ungrateful to ignore the immense treasure of insights that we inherit from them and that furthers us in our understanding of the Word today.

Then there are the *conciliar and other definitions of the Church*. All of them exist in order to protect the genuine meaning and depth of revelation from misinterpretations toward the right and left. It is strange: one can certainly say that they should be read in their historical context and that they use words and concepts of their time that are often not exactly our own, but I do not know of a single really convincing attempt to replace them with better formulations that are as rich in content. Of course, the Fathers of Chalcedon themselves knew that their short formula for the essence of Christ, "two natures, one person", is only a formal skeleton that must be covered with the whole flesh of Scripture in order to live. And of course what we mean today, by and large, by "person" is no longer the same as what they had in mind. And yet, the point then was not to philosophize about Christ but to sketch with simple words an outline of his full mystery: a single somebody who is true God and true man. One can further simplify what the formula attempts to express and say: two "whats" but one "who". The council says nothing about how this is possible, and all theological systems will not clarify the mystery into a concept of which one can gain an overview. But someone who wants to go beyond this outline that is formulated "in the manner of fishermen" (*piscatorie*) will probably fall back into one of the dubious steps that led up to it. This precisely does not prevent one from understanding Chalcedon, not as an "end", but as a "beginning": the beginning of a necessary attempt, never to be concluded, at understanding how in Christ the human and the divine are together "unmixed and unseparated". In all "definitions", one should remember above all that a segment is lifted out of a whole that belongs together and is examined, as it were, with the magnifying glass. For this reason, a later view can order what has been "defined" in this way into a larger context that does not really relativize it but "relationalizes" it, so to speak, by placing it into a frame of reference. This is obviously already the case in Chalcedon, which places the formula of Ephesus into a more comprehensive context; Vatican II did this also with Vatican I, which was broken off prematurely. In the later, new view of what has been defined, what becomes clear is less its conditioning by the time and circumstances than its real meaning that transcends time. The Council of Trent, too, did not mean to dogmatize Scholastic philosophy when it spoke of transubstantiation; it wanted to outline the mystery that "this" is no longer bread but the Body of Christ; and even in our "fisher-man's" everyday language, the word "substance" is still the one that comes closest to expressing this fact. Again, the council never intended to explain how the mystery occurs.

Thirdly and finally, the interpretation of the *moral obligations* of Christians that follow from the paradigm of Christ in each culturally changed period. We have already said that one should not carry the greater mobility of this sphere into the first area of interpretation. But before one can speak of this mobility, one has to consider thor-oughly, first, a certain unchangeable fundamen-tal human structure and, second, the character of scandal that the life of discipleship has. One must neither sacrifice the dignity of human nature to the all-devouring subjection of the world to tech-nology nor minimize the difference of Christians from the surrounding world under the pretext of "adapting" or of simplifying the apostolate. "Do not be conformed to this world" (Rom 12:2), live "blameless and innocent, children of God without blemish in the midst of a crooked and perverse generation, among whom you shine as lights in the world" (Phil 2:15). One can understand from this how cautious the Church must be in rein-terpreting moral principles in fringe areas, where perhaps a catastrophe that threatens mankind as a whole gives rise to something like an emergency that makes it unavoidable to accept a loss of clarity regarding what is required to follow Jesus.

To argue simply with "human rights" in such cases, rights in the name of which one can demand from the leadership of the Church what "everybody" considers unquestionably as "normal", would be fallacious and naïve. For in his baptism, the Christian died to the "old Adam" and rose with Christ, the new and eternal Adam, and has come under a new law, a law of freedom. We are explicitly told (1 Cor 7) that, though we have been newly created in Christ, we are still "in the flesh", and especially in married life we experience "division" between the new and the old aeon more painfully than in a decisively celibate life. But for Christians, marriage is a sacrament, which means above all a form, given as a gift to the spouses, of following Christ in his fruitful, purifying, complete self-surrender to his spouse, the Church. The Christian attitude and practice of married life receive their norm from here (Eph 5:22–33). For this reason, reinterpretations of Christian ethics are especially difficult in this area and must in no case be made lightly or forced by pressures.

Nobody will deny that here, as well as in other areas, the relation of the Christian to questions of his environment demands a continual dialogue between the laity (especially those competent in the questions) and the office in the Church. The condition of such a dialogue is simply that the whole

Church, laymen as well as clerics, stands in common obedience to Christ, the Head of the Church. Otherwise, all obedience in the Church is made impossible from the outset, and ecclesial authority would find no point of connection in order to be effective in a Christian sense. Paul stressed this most clearly in confrontation with his Corinthians who contested him. In order to be accepted at all by the community with his apostolic authority—which has the weakness of the Crucified and the vitality of the Risen—he must implore them: "Examine yourselves, to see whether you are holding to your faith. Test yourselves! Do you not realize that Jesus Christ is in you?—unless indeed you fail to meet the test! I hope that you will find out that we have not failed." And in case this self-assertion of the office should sound overbearing, the apostle adds: "We beg God that you may not do wrong—not that we may appear to have met the test, but that you may do what is right, though we may seem to have failed." Only if Christ speaks out of them, i.e., only if the whole body of the Church is an obedient organ of the Head, may the official authority express the wish to be humbled for the sake of the Lord. "For we cannot do anything against the truth", Paul concludes, "but only for the truth." Spiritual authority is powerless in the face of the disobedient and of those who are convinced of their own point of view. For this reason, "we are glad when we are weak and you are strong" (2 Cor 13:5–9).

DRAWING THE LINE

The consequence follows automatically once this unanimity of the Church is presupposed. If the Church (corresponding to the Incarnation of the Word) is something visible, she must also have visible limits. This says nothing about the final salvation of those who stand outside her boundaries; God wills "all men to be saved" (1 Tim 2:4). But it is also written that Peter should be concerned, not with what remains unknown to him, but with the flock appointed to him. "If it is my will that he remain until I come, what is that to you? Follow me" (Jn 21:22).

Paul presupposes this unanimity of the community when he has to draw a line and excommunicate a previous member for the sake of the Church's integrity (cf. 1 Cor 5:3–5, 9–13; 2 Cor 2:5–11). Hence the seemingly paradoxical statement: "[We are] ready to punish every disobedience, when your [the community's] obedience is complete" (2 Cor 10:6). John speaks even more severely: the one who has fallen away no longer has any part in the prayer of the Church (1 Jn 5:16); those who do not recognize the Son of the Father in Jesus distance themselves from the Church; in this way it becomes "plain that they all are not of us" (1 Jn 2:19). Of course, you should "convince some, who doubt; save some, by snatching them out of the fire"; in the case of those who do not let themselves be saved, compassion but distance is commanded (Jude 22–23). "If any one comes to you [as a community] and does not bring this doctrine [that Jesus is true God], do not receive him into the house or give him any greeting" (2 Jn 10). And again Paul: "If any one refuses to obey what we say in this letter, note that man, and have nothing to do with him, that he may be ashamed" (2 Thess 3:14). "Now we command you, brethren, in the name of our Lord Jesus Christ, that you keep away from any brother who is walking in idleness and not in accord with the tradition that you received from us" (2 Thess 3:6). To Titus: "As for a man who is factious, after admonishing him once or twice, have nothing more to do with him" (Titus 3:10). In the First Letter to Timothy, two who "have made shipwreck of their faith" are excommunicated (1 Tim 1:19–20). This universal practice goes back to the Gospel, where the command is given to show somebody his sin first privately; if this is fruitless, then in the presence of witnesses; and if he does not listen even then, in the presence of the Church; "but if he refuses to listen even to the Church, let him be to you as a Gentile and a tax collector" (Mt 18:15–17). The Church through the centuries followed this instruction that is so frequently repeated, though

often with means that cannot be sanctioned in the
light of the message of Christ. But it would go against
the entire New Testament to deny the Church in
principle the right and the duty of drawing a line
and to vilify this practice as "sniffing out heretics".
Of course, this is not to say that the social side of the
way original Christianity drew the line—breaking off
even common human intercourse—must be maintained literally today. What is essential is breaking off
the communion within the Church, above all sacramental communion. The "table of the Lord", as the
Church has always understood and practiced it, is not
a continuation of Jesus' "meals with sinners" but the
gift of an inner participation in his most holy attitude.
This is the reason for the washing of the feet and for
the prayer: "For their sake I consecrate myself, that
they also may be consecrated in truth" (Jn 17:19).
For this reason, Paul demands an examination of
conscience from everyone who approaches. The
table itself, and what it offers, demands distinction
and, thereby, separation, not in order to form a sect,
but in order to prepare the true apostles of Christ for
their mission.

After all, everybody is free to believe or not to
believe what he pleases. The freedom of religion
was solemnly proclaimed by the last council. If
someone cannot identify himself with the apostolic
faith of the Catholic Church, nobody hinders him
from distancing himself from it. What advantage
would he have from confessing this faith and at the
same time falsifying it for himself and others?

PARTIAL IDENTIFICATION

This is a new catchword that is said to fit the major-
ity of Catholics in our countries. Put differently,
those who have settled at the "periphery" are said
to be more numerous than those who, in contrast,
are called "integralists" in a derogatory sense.

To see here more clearly, one should look back
to the threefold gradation made above in the context
of "reinterpretation". The evaluation of the truths of
faith belonging to the first category may be decisive.
Many Christians today (as probably also in earlier
times) see the Creed's individual "articles of faith" as
isolated truths, some of which appeal to them so that
they gladly believe them, while others strike them as
strange or even hostile. These people lack the inner
insight into how closely the essential articulations
of the Christian faith belong together and how grievous the consequences are for the whole if one or
several are set aside.

Let us go through *the Creed in summary* fashion.
We confess God the *Father as maker* of heaven and
earth. One could doubt God's fatherliness if one
looks at the horrors of this world. The assertion

becomes bearable only if one adds what follows: that this God is not a god who looks on as a spectator from above and outside but one who gives his beloved Son to this world, even hands him over to execution, in order through him to bear the whole suffering of the world experientially in solidarity and to transfigure it from within. How would we know that God is a lover and a compassionate Father if Jesus Christ, as his co-essential Son ("Light from Light, true God from true God"), had not "made known" (Jn 1:18) to us his Heart: in words and deeds, in sovereignty and humility, in judgment upon sin and mercy to the sinner, in the fact that he gave us the Holy Spirit, the Spirit of the mutual love between Father and Son? For without the divine Spirit, our spirit could never have experienced anything of the mystery of God's depths (1 Cor 2:10–11). Only in the light of *Christ's life, Passion, and Resurrection* can one dare to assert that God is in himself eternal triune love, in himself and not only by the fact that he became man (and was thus previously not triune); not only by the fact that God gains an object of love in the world, for then he would not be "love". In the middle of the Creed, which deals with Father, Son, and Holy Spirit, there is the little sentence, "by the Holy Spirit was incarnate *of the Virgin Mary*". Could one not bracket at least this seemingly unimportant sentence? Why should this Jesus of Nazareth not have been begotten and born normally and as such

be the Word of God made man? Because, to put
it briefly, Jesus, who calls God "his Father" in a
unique and exclusive way, simply cannot have two
fathers (toward whom he would have to keep the
fourth commandment); and, further, because his
Mother must summarize the whole faith of Abraham and the Old Covenant in herself and transcend
it; because she may not offer any resistance to this
Incarnation of the Word in her womb and in her
whole spiritual-bodily being but must rather bring
to it her complete spiritual-bodily assent. For centuries, the Church reflected on the tender mystery
between this Child and this Mother, and she quite
logically arrived at the few sentences about Mary,
the humble handmaid who looked toward God.
The connection of these sentences with the triune
mystery of God and the true, concrete Incarnation
of the Son seemed undeniable to the Church. To
bracket them and pull them out of context would
be a tangible impoverishment of the faith. The central assertion that "for our sake [Jesus] was *crucified*"
follows in the Creed; "for us men and for our salvation" he had already come "down from heaven ...
and [become] man". This assertion is meaningful
only if the true divinity of Christ is certain. A mere
man, be he ever so gifted with grace, could never,
as Scripture says, bear away the sin of the world.
It follows from the preceding that God the Father,
who permitted him this work of atonement, raises
him from the dead and brings him into his glory and

makes him the judge and standard for the world that has been lifted into salvation.

It may be more difficult to assent in each single case to the characteristics of the Church of Jesus Christ that are included in confessing the Holy Spirit, for her historical appearance seems to contradict them all. Instead of being one, she is torn apart; instead of being holy, she is sinful many times over in her members; instead of being apostolic, she appears fallen away from her original ideal; instead of being catholic, all-encompassing, she appears to have become the particular Church gathered around Rome. And yet, in her form that can be deciphered only with difficulty, one can see her hidden nature shine through as if through a transparent medium. Through the cord wound from the three strands of word–office–sacrament, she holds fast, without swerving, to her apostolic origin, to the holiness given to her as a gift that at times expresses itself in shining examples, to her claim of maintaining the universal truth of the revelation of God in which the true values of all other Christian denominations and, indeed, of all religions can be integrated as parts into a whole, even though Catholics often realize little of the Catholic fullness. And in the strength of this fundamental, integrative capacity, she proves that, in spite of all divisions, she is the one Church.

She keeps the treasure of the sacramental gifts of Christ, not only baptism and the forgiveness of sins, but also the communication of holy things (*communio sanctorum*); that means above all the Eucharist, the Presence, mediated by the office, of Christ's effective salvation and of his existence as bodily salvation, through which we are given the hope that is most incomprehensible in human terms: the hope that our whole bodily being, despite its subjection to time and corruption, will find a dwelling in the eternal triune life of God, the creating Father, the redeeming Son, and the Spirit who gives us a share in the divine life.

This short survey of the Creed had only one purpose: to call to mind the way the mysteries of faith are woven into each other, a way that allows no selection from among them and in this sense no "partial identification" with one segment of the faith. Every Christian can make the same experiment with the texts of the Mass, whether it be the prayers and their great Catholic petitions or especially the four Eucharistic Prayers, each of which expresses the faith of the Church in its own way. Can I assent to these plain words according to their obvious meaning, or do I have to add mental restrictions and reservations to get over the texts? Do I experience the unity of the Church's faith through the millennia—for most of these prayers are ancient—or does it seem to me that the formulas are outdated in the light of modern enlightened consciousness?

Very often, of course, a Christian slips into such "partial identification", not because of the Creed, but because of some scandal in the Church that wounded him. It can be very difficult to get over such experiences. One opens one's heart without suspicion to some authority in the Church whom one hoped would be holy and sanctifying, and something evil was poured into it. "No wonder", says Paul, when speaking of false and insidious apostles who pretend to be apostles of Christ, "for even Satan disguises himself as an angel of light" (2 Cor 11:13–14). But even in such a case, the image of the true Church that the one so painfully wounded bears in himself should win out against the snare he encountered. Nothing is partial in Jesus; nor is anything partial in that Church which he desired and which, united with him, has in him her reality.

THE CROSS—FOR US

Without a doubt, at the center of the New Testament there stands the Cross, which receives its interpretation from the Resurrection. The Passion narratives are the first pieces of the Gospels that were composed as a unity. In his preaching at Corinth, Paul initially wants to know nothing but the Cross, which "will destroy the wisdom of the wise, and [thwart] the cleverness of the clever", which "is a stumbling block to Jews and folly to Gentiles". But "the foolishness of God is wiser than men, and the weakness of God is stronger than men" (1 Cor 1:19, 23, 25). Whoever removes the Cross and its interpretation by the New Testament from the center, in order to replace it, for example, with the social commitment of Jesus to the oppressed as a new center, no longer stands in continuity with the apostolic faith. He does not see that God's commitment to the world is most absolute precisely at this point—across a chasm.

It is certainly not surprising that the disciples were able to understand the meaning of the Cross only slowly, even after the Resurrection. The Lord himself gives a first catechetical instruction to the disciples at Emmaus by showing that this

incomprehensible event is the fulfillment of what
had been foretold and that the open question marks
of the Old Testament find their solution only here
(Lk 24:27). Which riddles? Those of the Covenant
between God and men in which the latter must
necessarily fail again and again: Who can be a match
for God as a partner? Those of the many cultic sacrifices that in the end are still external to man while
he himself cannot offer himself as a sacrifice. Those
of the inscrutable meaning of suffering that can fall
even, and especially, on the innocent, so that every
proof that God rewards the good becomes void.
Only at the outer periphery, as something that so
far is completely sealed, appear the outlines of
a figure in which the riddles might be solved. This
figure would be at once the completely kept and
fulfilled Covenant, even far beyond Israel (Is 49:5–
6), and the personified sacrifice in which at the same
time the riddle of suffering, of being despised and
rejected, becomes a light; for it happens as the vicar-
ious suffering of the just for "the many" (Is 52:13—
53:12). Nobody had understood the prophecy then,
but, in the light of the Cross and Resurrection of
Jesus, it became the most important key to the
meaning of the apparently meaningless.

Did not Jesus himself use this key at the Last Supper in anticipation? "For you", "for the many", his
Body is given up and his Blood is poured out. He
himself, without a doubt, foreknew that his will to
help these people toward God who are so distant
from God would at some point be taken terribly

seriously, that he would suffer in their place through this distance from God, indeed, this utmost darkness of God, in order to take it from them and to give them an inner share in his closeness to God. "I have a baptism to be baptized with; and how I am constrained until it is accomplished!" (Lk 12:50). It stands as a dark cloud at the horizon of his active life; everything he does then—healing the sick, proclaiming the kingdom of God, driving out evil spirits by his good Spirit, forgiving sins—all of these partial engagements happen in the approach toward the one unconditional engagement.

As soon as the formula "for the many", "for you", "for us", is found, it resounds through all the writings of the New Testament; it is even present before anything is written down (cf. 1 Cor 15:3). Paul, Peter, John: everywhere the same light comes from the two little words. What has happened? Light has for the first time penetrated into the closed dungeons of human and cosmic suffering and dying. Pain and death receive meaning. Not only that, they can receive more meaning and bear more fruit than the greatest and most successful activity, a meaning not only for the one who suffers but precisely also for others, for the world as a whole. No religion had even approached this thought.[1] The

---

[1] For what is meant here is something qualitatively completely different from the voluntary or involuntary scapegoats who offered themselves or were offered (e.g., in Hellas or Rome) for the city or for the fatherland to avert some catastrophe that threatened everyone.

great religions had mostly been ingenious methods of escaping suffering or of making it ineffective. The highest that was reached was voluntary death for the sake of justice: Socrates and his spiritualized heroism. The detached farewell discourses of the wise man in prison could be compared from afar to the wondrous farewell discourses of Christ. But Socrates dies noble and transfigured; Christ must go out into the hellish darkness of godforsakenness, where he calls for the lost Father "with prayers and supplications, with loud cries and tears" (Heb 5:7). Why are such stories handed down? Why has the image of the hero, the martyr, thus been destroyed? It was "for us", "in our place".

One can ask endlessly how it is possible to take someone's place in this way. The only thing that helps us who are perplexed is the certainty of the original Church that this man belongs to God, that "he truly was God's Son", as the centurion acknowledges under the Cross, so that finally one has to render him homage in adoration as "my Lord and my God" (Jn 20:28). Every theology that begins to blink and stutter at this point and does not want to come out with the words of the apostle Thomas or tinkers with them will not hold to the "for us". There is no intermediary between a man who is God and an ordinary mortal, and nobody will seriously hold the opinion that a man like us, be he ever so courageous and generous in giving himself, would be able to take upon himself the sin of another, let alone the sin of all. He can suffer death in the place of someone who is condemned to death. This would be generous, and it would spare the other person death at least for a time. But what Christ did on the Cross was intended in no way to spare us death but, rather, to revalue death completely. In place of the "going down into the pit" of the Old Testament, it became "being in paradise tomorrow". Instead of fearing death as the final evil and begging God for a few more years of life, as the weeping King Hezekiah does, Paul would like most of all to die immediately in order to "be with Christ" (Phil 1:23). Together with death, life is also revalued: "If we live, we live to the Lord, and if we die, we die to the Lord" (Rom 14:8).

But the issue is not only life and death but our existence before God and our being judged by him. All of us were sinners before him and worthy of condemnation. But God "made him to be sin who knew no sin, so that in him we might become the righteousness of God" (2 Cor 5:21). Only God in his absolute freedom can take hold of our finite freedom from within in such a way as to give it a direction toward him, an exit to him, when it was closed in on itself. This happened in virtue of the "wonderful exchange" between Christ and us: he experiences instead of us what distance from God is, so that we may become beloved and loving children of God instead of being his "enemies" (Rom 5:10).

Certainly God has the initiative in this reconciliation: *he* is the one who reconciles the world to
himself in Christ. But one must not play this down
(as famous theologians do) by saying that God is
always the reconciled God anyway and merely
manifests this state in a final way through the death
of Christ. It is not clear how this could be the fitting
and humanly intelligible form of such a manifesta-
tion. No, the "wonderful exchange" on the Cross
is the way by which God brings about reconciliation. It can only be a mutual reconciliation because
God has long since been in a covenant with us. The
mere forgiveness of God would not affect us in our
alienation from God. Man must be represented in
the making of the new treaty of peace, the "new
and eternal covenant". He is represented because
we have been taken over by the man Jesus Christ.
When he "signs" this treaty in advance in the name
of all of us, it suffices if we add our name under his
now or, at the latest, when we die.

Of course, it would be meaningless to speak of
the Cross without considering the other side, the
Resurrection of the Crucified. "If Christ has not
been raised, then our preaching is in vain and ...
your faith is futile and you are still in your sins.
Then those also who have fallen asleep ... have per-
ished. If for this life only we have hoped in Christ,
we are of all men most to be pitied" (1 Cor 15:14,
17–19). If one does away with the fact of the Resurrection, one also does away with the Cross, for

both stand and fall together, and one would then have to find a new center for the whole message of the Gospel. What would come to occupy this center is at best a mild father-god who is not affected by the terrible injustice in the world, or man in his morality and hope who must take care of his own redemption: "atheism in Christianity".

MARY–CHURCH–OFFICE

Someone who disregards the place of Mary in the history of salvation, as the Church has come to know it in her prayer and contemplation, will pay the price in the long run; he will sooner or later land in a feminism that demands the equality, which means in practical terms the identification, of woman and man.

The relationship of *mother and child* and that of *man and woman* are such deep mysteries and approaches to the divine mystery in the reality of creation that for someone who does not integrate them into redemption, the Incarnation cannot be complete. If one posits Joseph as the father of Jesus, then Jesus is necessarily brought down to the level of a mere "prophet". If the virginal motherhood is acknowledged but its theological significance for Mary contested (as in the case of Karl Barth), then Jesus remains an isolated meteorite that dropped from heaven, and his relation to the Church cannot possibly be seen in terms that are as concrete and realistic as Paul describes them (Eph 5). The Church remains an association of individual believers (as in Kierkegaard); she does not truly become the Bride of Christ.

Something else is characteristic of the Protestant deficiency: the absence of Mariology is parallel to the Lutheran rift between the law and Gospel that in the long run implies anti-Semitism. Let us now say all of this positively.

In Mary, as was said above, the *whole faith of Israel*, beginning with the unprecedented faith of Abraham, is gathered, a faith that tends toward Christ and remains a paradigm for Christians, as Hebrews 11 shows extensively and emphatically. How should all the extremely positive elements of the Old Covenant not be included in the establishing of the New Covenant that is expressly called the former's "fulfillment"? How could Christ enter into the history of salvation without letting all this positivity be given to him through his Mother? Certainly, in Mary's perfect act of faith that presupposes her freedom from any defect of hesitation due to original sin, the faith of Abraham is not only gathered but transcended, as the best blossom and richest fruit seem to transcend the power of the tree that produces them. And yet, all the yearning for salvation and all the obedience in faith present in the Fathers and all their "labor pains" for the Messiah have their share in the arrival of the Messiah. Quite rightly the exegetes see first of all the Old Testament community of salvation in the loudly crying *woman of Revelation*. But in the person of Mary, it actually brings forth its Redeemer, and from this point it becomes the Church of the New Testament, for the woman has further children who "bear testimony to Jesus" (Rev 12:17). Heaven and earth cooperate: "The LORD will give what is good, and our land will yield its increase" (Ps 85:12).

Woman, as *synagogue–Mary–Church*, is the inseparable unity of that which makes it possible for the Word of God to take on the being of the world, in virtue of the natural-supernatural fruitfulness given to her. As the active power of receiving all that heaven gives, she is the *epitome of creaturely power and dignity*; she is what God presupposes as the Creator in order to give the seed of his Word to the world. In no religion (not even in those of matriarchal cultures) and in no philosophy can woman be the original principle, since her fruitfulness, which appears more active and explicit in the sexual sphere than the fruitfulness of man, is always ordered to insemination. This is also true of Isis, Astarte, and Cybele. In the philosophy of antiquity, man appears for this reason as the number one and woman as the number two. Eve is drawn from Adam's side that his creaturely creative power may not be in vain. The following words of Paul must be placed into this cosmic context: "[Man] is the image and glory of God; but woman is the glory of man" (1 Cor 11:7). "Glory" (*doxa*) in the last part of the sentence can and must be understood as that through which man is glorified. God does not need Adam in order to have his glory in himself. Adam, however, is poor and fruitless if he does not have that in which he brings forth fruit bodily and spiritually, that which, as the principle of fruitfulness and as wife and mother, fructifies him. "For as woman was made from man, so man is now born of woman. And all things [man and woman] are from God" (1 Cor 11:12): from God who, as the Creator, bears in himself the archetype of man and woman but who is to be revered as "Father", since he always has priority in generating. At most one can say that the eternal Son in whom the Father created all things is, as "wisdom", in a certain way "feminine" in relation to the Father, but he must represent the Father in the world by his Incarnation, and this he can do only as a man.

But he does so as a man who comes *from* woman (the Old Covenant community of salvation, which finds its peak in Mary) and is again fruitful *in* woman (in the same community of salvation that *becomes the Church in Mary*).

Completing the prior unity of Old Covenant and Mary, one must thus pay attention now to the connection between Mary and the Church. The assent given to the angel by the "lowly handmaid" on whom God has looked graciously is the fundamental act of her entire life. It therefore includes everything that God wants to realize through her and through her Child: even the sword that perpetually pierces her, even the unbearable Cross. At the Presentation in the Temple, she fundamentally offers and returns her Child to God. On the Cross, this return—in the same godforsakenness as the Son: "Woman, behold your son!"—becomes a secret but indispensable part of the New Creation or birth. Both things are true: the Church comes to be from the "breathing out" of the Spirit in Jesus' death and from his opened side, *and* she comes to be in virtue of the fact that the feminine assent to all that God wills becomes the inexhaustible fruitfulness of the new Eve. It is the Church that Paul (Eph 5:27) calls the "*immaculata*", which, after all, she is truly and literally on earth only in her archetype, Mary. The Cross (to which Easter and Pentecost belong inseparably) is the fulfillment of all the nuptial spirit between man and woman and, indeed, between heaven and earth.

This *nuptial spirit* remains the innermost mystery of the Church, a blissful and at the same time a painful mystery since it originates perpetually in the actuality of the Cross. The New Testament (not just the Letter to the Hebrews) describes Christ's suffering on the Cross as the fulfillment and surpassing of all previous sacrifices. Thus it is pointless to argue about whether or not the word "sacrifice" is still appropriate for it. It is best to say (with Augustine) that the only sacrifice that is fully valid and fills out this concept completely is Christ's giving himself for us to God, and all other Jewish and pagan sacrifices are only shadows that point to this. But the assent of the Mother, and of the other holy women under the Cross, is silently included in this transcendent sacrifice from which, in the most painful labor, the Church is born.

Situated within this comprehensive femininity of the Church is the *Eucharistic mystery* that Jesus entrusts in advance to his apostles and also the power to bind and loose in relation to sinners that he gives to them on Easter. This "within" was expressed by the contemplative Middle Ages and by the Eastern Church in innumerable images: the Spirit that descends on Pentecost upon the Church touches Mary each time at the center of the apostles, Mary as the epitome of *Ecclesia*, who, under the Cross, caught the Blood from Christ's wounded side in her chalice.

Men are to carry out the office in the Church; in so doing, they are not to *be* Christ but merely to represent him. It is part of the nature of the office that it *merely* represents, so much so that it can speak, not its own words, but the words of Christ: "This is *my* Body"; "*I* absolve you". *It is completely unthinkable that Mary should speak such words.* For under the Cross, she did not represent the sacrifice of her Son, but—in being set aside and given away to another son—she was a silent, invisible part of this sacrifice. For she, the woman, *is* the Church that gives her assent, and everyone in the Church has a part in this assent. Even the man, even the priest, is in this respect feminine, Marian.

The woman who would strive for the male role in the Church thus strives for something "less" and denies the "more" that she is. This can be over-looked only by a feminism that has lost the sense for the mystery of sexual difference, which has func-tionalized sexuality and attempts to increase the dignity of woman by bringing about her identifi-cation with man. No proof that in earlier Christian theology woman was philosophically underrated (because of the influence of Greek philosophy) can invalidate what has been said. Besides, the Chris-tian courtly culture of the Middle Ages by far sur-passed in influence the philosophical underrating of woman (mainly in clerical and monastic circles) by its almost mystical esteem for woman.

A final mystery remains to be uncovered. If the Cross is a sacrifice, or rather the only perfect sac-rifice, and if in the Mass we become present anew to Christ's work of salvation to the point of being allowed to receive his Body that is given up and his Blood that is poured out, then it should be self-evident that we are thereby *drawn into* his attitude of self-giving and thus into *his sacrificial attitude*. This would be true even if we wanted to look upon the Mass as a mere "meal". But two thoughts lead beyond this aspect.

First of all, Jesus hands over his sacrifice at the Last Supper to his disciples in order that they may perform it in imitation: "Do this in memory of me." He himself passes from his active life to the passivity of suffering, of being overtaxed, in which one can no longer be active oneself but must suffer whatever happens. And thus he can hand over to his disciples the active aspect of his readiness for God: he gives his sacrifice to them so that they, too, may have something to offer to God. Anyone to whom this seems incredible should look at the parallel on the evening of Easter. Christ, who has "merited" the greatness of heaven's absolution by bearing sin, does not now absolve his disciples who left him but places absolution into their hands so that they may carry it out as his representatives. A first answer is thereby given to the question, so frequently discussed today, of whether the Mass is a sacrifice. Yes, it is a sacrifice: it is Christ's sacrifice, which he places into the hands of his Church so that she in turn has something to offer to the Father: the only thing of value, the sacrifice of Christ.

A second consideration, however, is hidden behind this and is not difficult to discover after what has been said. The Church that "joins" in the sacrifice of Christ did so in her archetype under the Cross once and for all; and what she did there was the highest thing, the most difficult and the most closely united to the sacrifice of Christ that is at all thinkable. But this consideration receives weight only if one maintains that the Church is in her archetype the woman: she is Mary, not merely a sociological "people", but the chosen people that is descended from Abraham and is gathered together for the first time in Mary in order to become again a people from her and from her Son. At the point at which the Church gives what is most precious to her to the Father for the salvation of the world, the gesture of sacrifice (expressed in many ways in the Eucharistic Prayer) is deepened in unprecedented fashion. And it is also clearer now why the community that "sacrifices" here is not a community of sinners (which is glad when another atones in its place) but the community of "saints", which purified itself at the beginning of the celebration through the confession and absolution of sins.

Here, and nowhere else, the indispensability of Mariology becomes evident not only for the doctrine of the nature and work of Christ but equally for the understanding of what the Church is in truth.

INTERCOMMUNION

Something can be said here about the painful subject of the intercommunion, longed for but still not possible, between Christian communities that are not united in their faith. The differences are concentrated precisely at the point where the mystery of the Eucharist stands, which is in our understanding the central mystery, the one that provides the ultimate foundation of the Church and keeps her in existence.

Many laymen may be convinced of the role of the Eucharist, but without sufficiently considering the presuppositions and consequences of this conviction. Thus one cannot blame them when they think that intercommunion can bridge the remaining differences and help, perhaps through the effect of its grace, to make them disappear. But if the sacrament is understood differently on both sides, it cannot produce unity; nor can its function be to bring about a reconciliation (magically, as it were? *ex opere operato*?) that can be produced only through the conscious deed of the persons involved. "Leave your gift before the altar and go; first be reconciled to your brother, and then come and offer your gift" (Mt 5:24).

Again, many will say: "But I am already reconciled with him. I have nothing against him. Both of us received the same baptism and believe that we encounter Christ in the celebration of the Last Supper. Is that not the essential?" In this case, all the rest that still separates us would be unessential, and it could be passed over as practically unimportant. But do not the numerous ecumenical discussions today precisely about the Eucharist show that we have come so close to each other theoretically that the similarity clearly outweighs the difference? Then what hinders the people of God, considering the urgency of unification stressed by all sides, from drawing the practical consequences?

The earnest striving for unification in ecumenical discussions must not be denied in any way, nor must the usefulness of its objective clarifications. The question remains whether the important aspects of the question of the Eucharist that divided the Church in the sixteenth century can appear so harmless today that they dwindle to trivialities. These aspects are above all the following three. What was set out in the previous section helps to make them clearer.

1. Jesus' distribution of himself—"This is the Blood of the Covenant poured out for you"—is clearly an anticipatory sign and inclusion of his Cross. Paul expresses this by saying that the one who receives the sacrament proclaims the death of

Christ. The sacrament that was instituted "on the night before he suffered" does not change its character after Easter, and it does not mediate just any encounter with a timeless Jesus; such an encounter takes place in the Christian's entire life of faith, in each prayer, in each Christian encounter with a fellowman. The point is the conscious reception of the One who for us (by bearing our sin) went into the death of our godforsakenness, the One who, according to the splintering of sinners, splintered himself completely into their egotisms—far beyond the myth of Orpheus—in order to bring back what was lost. Do we know (here and on the other side) that we encounter the One who is given up into our abyss, the Lord who is kneeling before our soiled feet? Do we adore him as such?

2. The Catholic Church will never be able to abandon the idea that Jesus entrusted his powers of consecration and of the absolution from grievous guilt to an office in the Church that was first carried out by the "apostles" and then explicitly passed on to others who in turn are to pass it on: "This is why I left you in Crete, that you might amend what was defective and appoint elders in every town as I directed you" (Titus 1:5). This order appears completed even in the earliest postapostolic writings (Letter of Clement, circa 96; Letters of Ignatius, circa 115), and the Church cannot go back beyond this order to possible but more or less hypothetical community structures that formed under the

eyes of the apostles and with their approbation. Full communion of churches—and the Eucharist is the expression of the full, not of a partial, communion—presupposes communion, both visibly embodied and spiritually acknowledged, in the office of the Church, of which one cannot say (as some Catholic theologians do) that it can be changed in its essential structure by the Church herself. For it is essentially and permanently a gift of Christ *to* the Church, which is permitted to be what she is by virtue of this gift.

This must be maintained centrally, and it is neither possible nor permissible for us to relativize the normal structure of the Church in its validity on the basis of speculations about what God's grace is able to do in cases of need and at the border, as it were, and in which communities of faith the Lord of the Church can make himself present.

3. Finally, one must look at the mystery that we attempted to outline in the context of Mary's role, the mysterious but indubitable fact that the Church that is "passive" (and in this sense joins in the sacrifice) is integrated into the event of the Cross. The Eucharist is in no case a mere "memorial meal"; it certainly contains an inclusion of the community in the event of the death (and Resurrection) of Jesus, however differentiated and gradated the description of this mystery must be. The previous section attempted to show how this "being co-sacrificed" and "joining in the sacrifice" can be conceived.

The Eucharist is in its core at the same time a wonderful and painful mystery. It would be good if both sides that press for common communion remained aware of this and, by renouncing superficial and overly hasty unifications, experienced something of the pain that is contained in this sacrament in Jesus' self-abandonment for the sake of unification.

OFFICE OF UNITY

If one asks whether the office is present in the Creed, the answer is: certainly, above all in *"unam"*, which stands before *"sanctam, catholicam"*, and finally *"apostolicam ecclesiam"*. The Church could never be "one" if a visible principle of unity were not instituted in her, for we sinners always tend toward separation and sectarianism. And only what is united in this way can be catholic, i.e., all-encompassing, whereas our personal horizon can see and live only a part. Therefore, an *objective sanctity* must belong to this principle of unity that is the apostolic constitution of the Church—the college of the Twelve with Peter as the unifying center—corresponding to its being instituted by Christ and accompanied by him. *Subjective sanctity*, on the other hand, as it is fully embodied in the Church only by Mary, cannot by itself be a sufficient mark of the community of Christ. Christians should strive for this sanctity that consists in the love of God and neighbor, but when could they show this lived love to the world as the incontrovertible seal of genuineness?

Thus the four characteristics that were enumerated (they certainly do not exhaust the nature of the Church) in no way exist next to each other but exist, rather, in each other. But they do so only under the assumption that the "unity", which is the central mark of the Church's representation of God and the all-inclusive mark of catholicity that protects in each case the whole revelation and can integrate into itself every value of the world, lies also in its visible ecclesial structure—in an office with *one* center, the successor of Peter—so that all fragmentary striving for holiness occurs within this structure of unity.

For this is *the great pity with the ecumenical movement*, that the discussion partner of the Catholic Church can never be "one" but only splintered. While individual Protestants are for the recognition of the *Augustana* by the Catholic Church, others are certain to be against it. Even among themselves they cannot agree on its importance. Even in the case of the Orthodox, if individual authorities engage in talks with Rome, none of them can speak in a binding way, not even for his independently headed church. Another group will take the opposite position. Certainly the non-Catholic communities possess unifying elements in themselves: Scripture, for example, or a certain period or form of tradition. But we already saw in how many ways objectively Scripture can be interpreted, even without considering the subjective limitation of each interpreter. And the principle of tradition remains ambiguous, too, since it carries many heterogeneous elements

and since, in addition, it is questionable if, after separation from Rome, it can count as the full, living
tradition. More of this later; let us return now to the
issue within the Church.

The visible summary of the apostolic collegiality
in the Petrine ministry must not, of course, be confused or equated with the principle of unity that
stands at the foundation of the Church as such: this
principle is and remains the spiritual Christ. The
pope is not the subjective holiness of the Church,
nor does he found her unity; he merely administers
what has already been founded. But he can do so
only if, in the believers' common loving obedience
to Christ and in Christian love, the spiritual lati-
tude without which he cannot carry out his office
is granted to him as the one instituted by Christ.
If Christians are to love and seek unity above all
else, then they must permit the ecclesial principle,
whose office it is to maintain this unity, to carry
out its office. *An anti-Roman sentiment*, even if it
would make an appeal to the principle of apostolic
collegiality, *is most deeply anti-Catholic.* For its purpose is to pursue some imaginary unity by bypassing the office that has been instituted by Christ and
is responsible for this unity. Thus it creates inner
schisms in the Church that eventually push to the
fore. The Church is so much one in Christ that
the pope cannot carry out his function of unity if
all the faithful are not as obedient in the Spirit to
Christ as Christ was in the Spirit to the Father. If

the relationship of the believers to the bearers of office—the pope, the bishops, and priests—is not filled with the lifeblood of love, then one pushes their office into a bureaucracy that one deplores and criticizes without considering one's share of responsibility in it.

On the other hand, one cannot demand from the objective holiness of the office, even the papal office, that it should exemplify for believers the entire subjective holiness of the Church as it stems from Christ and his Spirit and as the *ecclesia immaculata* (Eph 5:27), namely Mary, embodies it. Equating the two and letting the credibility of the office depend on the personal holiness of its bearer is the most disastrous of the heresies combatted by Augustine, that of Donatism. In the sects of all ages, it flares up again. The bearer of the office should strive for credibility; but in the universal ecclesial love that is also directed toward the office as such, he should be supported by those who are indebted to him for the distribution of the Word and the sacraments and the unification of community, diocese, and the entire Church. Jesus' words to Peter, "When you have turned again, strengthen your brethren", concern all Christians in a corresponding way, for the bearers of the office are also their brothers, including the pope, who can bear his excessively heavy burden only if he is borne by all. He must perhaps be emboldened in love to continue to carry his cross with courage and humility and to resist the temptation to shift it to another's shoulders under the pretext of collegiality.

Such necessary encouragement is something much more serious than mere cheering, on the one hand, and sneering criticism, on the other. Both lack the consciousness of a loving share in the responsibility for the unity and holiness of the Church. Possibly cheering is a naïve expression of the decision to share in responsibility; possibly criticism is an expression, gone awry, of the same decision. Between these, there should be a commitment, well considered in faith, to this principle of unity that serves only as a representative—for only God in Christ is the unity—but is indispensable in this service.

AUTHORITY

In Christ, nature and behavior coincide. He is the Son of God and behaves as such. He speaks and acts with divine power and authority, never merely to rule, but to serve, even where he shows himself as ruler, to help the others (*auctoritas* comes from *augere*, to further something in its growth).

In this unity of being and behavior, he reveals God, who is absolute authority, as omnipotence, an authority that he still never manifests outside of his selfless love and goodness. This is true even within God, where each Divine "Person" exists, lives, and thinks completely for the sake of the others; it also holds for God's relationship to the world.

In the same *unity of being and behavior*, Jesus wants to be the paradigm for everybody who has authority in the human world. Even the authority that is founded in the order of creation must orient itself to this pattern. Parents have authority in their being the begetters of the child, but they must manifest it by working for the true development of the child's life. Similarly, a teacher has authority through his knowledge, which he must communicate to his students in service. An attorney, a doctor, anyone who has learned a profession must place his capability at the service of the community. The state as a whole has the highest worldly authority, but it is oriented to the furthering of justice for all and the well-being of each. This universal law in the worldly sphere offers a true preliminary understanding of what authority can be in the Church of Christ.

In the state and in society, because of human sinfulness, authority is often insisted upon as an objective possession of power without the corresponding subjective attitude of service. Jesus, on the other hand, always urges his community to realize the unity of spiritual authority and the corresponding spiritual attitude. "Let the greatest among you become as the youngest, and the leader as one who serves" (Lk 22:26 par.; 1 Cor 9:19f.; 2 Cor 4:5; Gal 5:13, etc.). And here the service goes to the point of the Cross in following Christ. This is explicit when Peter is given his authority: immediately, without a pause or gap, his own crucifixion is predicted to him (Jn 21:18f.).

Just as we earlier distinguished objective and subjective holiness, so now being and behavior, *objective and subjective authority*, form *the two sides of the one ecclesial authority*. The transfer of apostolic authority (through the "laying on of hands": cf. 2 Tim 1:6) intrinsically and urgently demands the corresponding attitude of service that orients itself by Christ.

Paul, who is completely expropriated for Christ, sings the praises of the "glory" of the ecclesial office, which he sees completely within this unity and discipleship (2 Cor 3:1–6, 10). In his view, the objective holiness of ecclesial authority demands the corresponding subjective holiness in order to reveal its true being.

The bearers of ecclesial offices are for the most part not perfect saints. The Christian people understand this and forgive it for the most part, although they continually look for true priests who live according to their spiritual authority. They know very well that a priest does not serve in the same way as an attorney or a doctor does, during office hours, but rather with his entire existence, which is expropriated for the Church. For this reason, the people often understand priestly celibacy more deeply and think it more self-evident than do many clerics, especially today. For this reason, they also have a fine sense for the gradations of spiritual existence, depending on whether a priest subjectively strives more or less to correspond to his objective authority.

The people know that the objective power of celebrating the Eucharist and giving absolution from grievous sins is independent of the personal holiness or unholiness of the priest. But they know just as well that the capacity to preach in the right Christian spirit and to teach religion, and even more the skill to further people in their striving for God, depend upon the priest's genuine prayer and genuine asceticism. His authority in relation to the faithful increases together with his humility. Part of this humility will always consist in having a healthy, not slavish, but faithful ecclesial sense that can combine docility with independent imagination. And corresponding to the Rules for Thinking with the Church in Ignatius' Exercises, if there is criticism to be made of institutions or persons in the Church, he will do so, not theatrically in public, but in the place where remedies can be applied.

CRITICAL OBEDIENCE

The office, as we said, does not dispense the individual believer from sharing in responsibility: for holiness, of course, but also for catholicity, so that he must criticize all particularism, even if it is proclaimed by theologians or from the pulpit. He must do so in the name of his better knowledge of the whole of truth that he knows from Scripture, tradition, and the liturgy. It becomes obvious here that the office is only one aspect of the whole and also that bearers of an office—individuals or groups, perhaps entire bishops' conferences—can be quite fallible, just as the pope speaks infallibly only in certain precisely defined situations. It is difficult to draw the line between the ordinary magisterium of all the bishops, the orthodoxy of which is guaranteed, and the fallibility of single bishops and bishops' conferences (not to speak of ordinary priests and vicars). The Christian laity's sense of faith (*sensus fidelium*) must always be alert. It must become restless, for example, when something is proclaimed in a sermon that does not correspond to the Creed or the Canon of the liturgy.

Modern forms of organization that penetrate into the Church often have a two-edged effect in her because the Church is not a community of inner-worldly pattern. The bishops' conferences, which are as such no theological authority, can meaningfully take care of common procedures in entire countries, but they contain the imminent danger that the individual bishop, the true theological authority, may hide behind his colleagues and no longer dare to take measures on his own responsibility. It is even worse when, as is the case in some countries, the conferences set up administrative bodies composed of so-called experts that should advise the bishops but that in reality terrorize them as pressure groups.[1] Even today, the same ambivalence is obvious in various "councils" that express shared responsibility ("democratically"). On the one hand, besides their own creative contributions, they make known the mentality of the times, including that within the Church, to the officials who necessarily have to consider this mentality in their final decision. But, on the other hand, it will in most cases *depend upon the quality of the pastor or the bishop whether parish, pastoral, diocesan, and other councils are beneficial or detrimental to the life of the Church.* For the one advised, the multiplication of such councils can become a veritable spider

---

[1] One can take as an example the impotence of the individual bishop in France in relation to his seminarians, who are educated in interdiocesan seminaries that are exclusively subject to a commission superior to all dioceses.

web that paralyzes him no less than worldly power
bound the bishops in earlier times. Just as then, the
papacy becomes the last place of refuge and support
of freedom for the ones who are thus entangled.
In addition, there is the fact that many bishops—
again, not to speak of pastors and vicars—are being
unsettled by loudly proclaimed "progressive" theologies. The old truths of faith appear to them so
undermined that they take refuge in empty com-
monplaces or merely sociological "pastoral care",
letting the faithful starve for any furtherance in the
authentic faith. On the parish level, on the pretext of coming closer to the people, the liturgy
is often reduced to the level of children's Sunday
school. The earnestness and the inner joy of the
common celebration is marred for the faithful by
a false familiarity and chumminess. Sermons repeat
again and again what the people have known for a
long time. As a result, a responsible Christian feels
underestimated and insulted and finally stays away.

Today the people of God thirst for spiritual drink
in a world that is ever more secularized and emptied
of God. They want to find teachers of silence, of
recollection, of prayer; and instead they find busy
clerics and often religious who have gotten stuck in
postconciliar confusions and antiauthoritarian dis-
putes, endlessly struggling for their own identity.
For this reason, many depart and seek what they
have a right to in places where they cannot find it:
from teachers of Eastern meditation, who may be

able to give them psychological comfort but never the encounter with the living and loving God of Jesus Christ.

Those searching people of God must not allow their sense of what is Catholic to be dulled; instead, they must realize their responsibility, and, in the hour when many pastors fall silent or even fail, the laymen must raise their cry of protest in the name of the complete Creed in which they were baptized.

> If those in the Church who are responsible for the faith fail individually or collectively, then it is in no way a sign of infidelity on the part of the believers, but on the contrary a sign of fidelity, to criticize and not to accept what this or that priest or even bishop or group of bishops teaches, if it is clearly contrary to what the pope, the councils, and the whole tradition of bishops down to us have taught. The obedience of the faithful must thus always be an illumined obedience and an obedience that is directed through human beings to Christ alone. If those who represent Christ put themselves in open opposition to him, to the whole tradition of the Church, and to those who are her surest representatives today, then one should not hesitate to resist them: to resist them respectfully at first and, if they do not understand or accept these criticisms, then firmly and to their face.[2]

[2] Louis Bouyer, *Le Métier de théologien: Entretiens avec Georges Daix* (Paris: Éd. France-Empire, 1979), 139–40.

TRADITIONALISM

But surely protest has existed for a long time in those groups that set themselves off to the right, partly in open opposition to the last council in the name of the previous tradition, partly at the edge of the Church, supporting themselves on whatever they can: on the obvious mistakes of the progressivists, on the proven old forms of the liturgy and of piety, and, not last, on numerous private revelations, whether they are acknowledged or (very often) not by the official Church.

These private revelations, mainly of Mary, some even of Christ, but also of the saints, compensate a number of groups for the lack of vitality that they cannot but feel in their rigid clinging to the forms of the past. Some of these revelations are full of threats for the future or demand the precise performance of works of atonement. Some show through their wealth of words and poverty of substance that a possibly genuine inspiration was received and made unclear by a turbid spiritual medium.

The oscillating between these extremes—obstinate insistence on old forms and the insistence of those who "know better" on the will of heaven—shows a lack of center and balance. The *ecclesia apostolica* and *sancta* is stressed, but the protesting splinter group wants to be at the same time the *una*, which is impossible, and the *catholica*, which a mere opposition, of its essence, cannot be. The most worrisome thing in the situation of the Church today may be that the left wing, which is quite chaotic but strong in the media, is confronted on the right by a large number of diligent but more or less introverted sectlike formations, all of which, of course, claim to be in the center but that hinder the formation of a superior center that embodies living tradition in a living way.

One gives or takes offense, as Guardini defined it once, if one asserts with penultimate reasons that one is right. Such penultimate reasons are the flagrant misuse of the new liturgical order by a great number of priests, while the ultimate reason still speaks for the Church of the council and against the traditionalists. The Mass was in urgent need of renewal, especially in regard to the active participation of all the faithful in the sacred act, which was a matter of course in the first centuries. Perhaps, as Fr. Louis Bouyer (who was just quoted) and Cardinal Ratzinger have stressed, one could for a certain period have continued to tolerate the old preconciliar form of the Mass (in which many basic things had been being changed since the time of Pius V). This form would then have passed away in a natural manner. What the traditionalists do not consider is that almost everything "new" that was added to the Missal of Paul VI stems from the oldest tradition of the liturgy; that the chief liturgical prayer, the Roman Canon, has remained unchanged; that the reception of the Host standing and in the hand was customary until the ninth century and that the Fathers of the Church attest that the faithful touched their eyes and ears with the Host in blessing before they consumed it. We should not forget, says Ratzinger, "that not only our hands are impure but also our tongue"—James describes it as our most sinful member (Jas 3:2–12)—"and also our heart.... It is the greatest daring, and at the same time an expression of the merciful goodness of God, that not only our hand and tongue but also our heart is allowed to touch him."[1]

Traditionalism bases itself on forms that rest on no living theology and philosophy and can for this reason claim no convincing validity today. Of course, the situation is different in different areas. It is one thing if in one country whole circles with their publications resentfully set themselves apart; it is different if high-spirited laymen in a different country fight against a progressive clergy by forming intensive prayer groups, by furthering radiantly influential houses for spiritual exercises, and

[1] *Eucharistie—Mitte der Kirche: Vier Predigten* (Munich: Erich Wewel, 1978), 45.

by composing edifying circulars. Here the true spirit has a chance to win against the Goliath of a powerfully organized bureaucratic letter. Here the so-called "right" approaches the only center from which the wished-for conciliar renewal can occur, the only one from which a theology can be constructed that is open to the uncurtailed revelation as well as to the needs of the time, the only one that, above the left and the right that have become incapable of dialogue, can give the Word of God new power among men.

ECUMENISM

What was just said provides the main postulate for the ecumenical dialogue necessary today, whether it be with the Churches of the East or with those that originated in the Reformation. Certainly, the split Church makes an unconvincing impression on the world; we must do everything to eliminate the scandal of schisms. But a Catholic Church that is split internally makes an impression on the Christian partner in dialogue that is no less unconvincing. *We are ripe for dialogue only if we have the certainty that we can manifest in the Church the unity and fullness of what is Catholic.* Anyone who works in order that the Catholic identity may find itself lays the foundation for a meaningful ecumenical dialogue.

For Catholics, this dialogue has two aspects, which must be seen simultaneously. On the one hand, the non-Catholic Christian communities stressed certain basic evangelical truths and kept them in their exodus from the Catholic Church, in which these truths were obscured and not reinserted with sufficient balance by the extreme contrary positions that were taken during the subsequent confrontations (catchword: "Counterreformation"). In this case, Catholics must listen to those who point out a piece of the totality of faith that is missing or not sufficiently realized. On the other hand, a member of the Catholic Church must be aware that his "separated brothers" can alert him only to things that have always rested in the fullness of his faith, things that were merely lost or forgotten through negligence or guilt. If this guilt is admitted, the claim to Catholic totality is possible without arrogance.

In no case can ecclesial unity be gained by theological compromises, such as ignoring the Catholic "surplus" that is considered unimportant, e.g., the unity of the office that stems from the primitive Church or the position of woman in the work of salvation. For all the communities that left the Catholic Church rest, inasmuch as they are separated, on more or less drastic negations of elements that belong to the organic unity of the tradition of faith. Theological sensitivity but also an ethical attitude are required of the Catholic in order to show others in Christian love that elements subtracted by them really belong to the unity. He must be able to show that the points at issue are a relative but indispensable part of the apostolic Creed. One brings about unity with Protestants, not by abolishing the dogmas concerning Mary or denying the apostolic succession, but by the proper integration of these truths into the comprehensive christological-trinitarian whole. Unity with the Orthodox is gained, not by giving up the true primacy of the successor of Peter,

but by its being lived in a credible way in the spirit
of the Gospel.

It is very difficult to bring about insight into
the necessity of abandoned elements in the case of
non-Catholics, since they look upon the Catholic
"surplus" as not merely unevangelical, dispensable,
and leading to abuses but above all as outdated anyway by modern secularization. Enlightened exegesis contributes to the support of this opinion by
claiming that it can show the secondary character of
many Catholic "overgrowths", and Catholic exegesis has a worrisome tendency toward such supposed
proofs. Then what is advocated is the removal of
secondary and un-Christian scandals in order to let
the only true scandal, that of the Cross of Christ and
his Resurrection, shine forth.

Relying on this apparent consensus, clerics above
all are seeking today, in high-spirited carelessness,
to realize "ecumenism from below" by practices
in their liturgies that lack every internal theological basis and external official permission. They want
thereby to help the all-too-hesitant office "find its
legs". But as much as cooperation, common prayer,
and common listening to Scripture and the sources
of the Church are to be wished for, and as true
as it is that everything must be done to decrease
hostilities and misunderstanding among Christians,
to the same extent every overhaste harms the true
concern. The unity envisioned by the ones who
push forward in this way is much too cheap and

superficial to correspond to the comprehensive fullness of divine revelation. Like the incarnate Word,
the Church (which is inseparable from him) has a
clearly delineated form; she is not like a pebble that
has been ground down and made formless in the
debris of a river.

POLITICAL THEOLOGY

From the beginning of the Church's history, it has been obvious that Christian ethics and mission in the world also have a political and, thus, a social dimension. Even during the time of the persecution of Christians by the Roman empire, Christians felt responsible in their prayer and living commitment for its well-being. Some even believed that the empire still existed solely because of Christian intercession. From Constantine on through the whole Middle Ages, Christendom had simultaneously an ecclesial and a political form. Both aspects were continually woven into each other in painful-beneficial tension. Abuses were not lacking: appropriation of worldly power by men of the Church, usurpation of ecclesial privileges by princes. Fusions of throne and altar lasted well beyond the time of absolutism. The nineteenth century, seemingly a period of the Church's retreat from political life, produced perhaps more true political fighters than the twentieth. The social encyclicals urged anew the political responsibility of Christians, so that one can point to them today in order to reject the claim of a new wave of political theology that it is taking this responsibility seriously for the first time.

But the terrible, ever-worsening social conditions, especially those of Latin America, have given
the call to this responsibility such urgency that a
previously unknown radicality is being demanded.
The existing need not only justifies the alarm of
everyone's conscience, those of the oppressed
poor as well as those of the oppressing owners of
estates, mines, and factories; it appears to justify
also a politicizing transformation of personal piety
and, for this purpose, a redefinition of Christ as
the liberator of the poor and oppressed (cf. Lk
4:18). It makes no difference if the oppressors call
themselves Christians or not. People appeal to
the harsh social preaching of prophets like Amos,
Micah, and Isaiah, who measured the value of a
rich Jew's religiosity according to his behavior to
the poor. Considering the criteria used by Christ
(Mt 25) in judging a Christian life, the "works of
mercy", it is not apparent why such an application of the standards of the Old Testament in the
New Testament should be outdated or forbidden
in today's Church.

The justified claims of the theology that calls
itself political cannot be rejected. Yet this theology
is fixed between two spheres of reality that embrace and
limit or relativize it: the sphere of world economics
and world politics and the comprehensive sphere
of New Testament theology. Its horizon remains
largely national and limited to one continent, but
the present problems cannot be solved within such

a horizon. It remains attached to the all-too-simple ideology of a dualism of oppressors and oppressed, whereas the situation (some flagrant cases excepted) is more complicated than that: most oppressors are in turn oppressed by others.

And in no way can the whole theology of the New Testament—its theology of the Cross and Resurrection—be reduced to political theology. The Cross of Christ, his godforsakenness, and his death are more than the mere continuation of his moral preaching and his solidarity with the poor and disadvantaged. That Jesus was no political zealot is acknowledged by every unbiased person today; that he concerned himself also with the rich and noble and even with tax collectors (who were for the most part "oppressors") is undeniable. He saw the ethical-political sphere in the wider context of bringing the kingdom of God, the final access to which opens up only through Cross and Resurrection. He failed in his extremely active struggle for the conversion of the earthly Israel whose Messiah he was. But beyond this failure, the "hour" was waiting for him, the hour that turns everything around: his Passion, through which he finally drew all to himself, not in an earthly-political, but in an eschatological way. "When you have done all that is commanded you, say, 'We are unworthy servants'" (Lk 17:10): Jesus may have been the first to have spoken these words to the Father. And the apparent meaninglessness of the Cross was, despite all appearances to the contrary, the fulfillment of his entire earthly struggle.

Political struggle is given as a charge to the Christian. But he must know that the kingdom of God is not established (in Marxist fashion) within the structures of this world.

APOCALYPSE

The Apocalypse, the conclusion of Christian revelation—every age of the Church has experienced its pertinence for itself by using various methods of interpretation. Our era can experience with great immediacy, bypassing many of these methods, that it stands under the apocalyptic signs and images.

One thing becomes very clear in the structure of the book that is so full of riddles. Even though terrible things happen to the world when the first seals are broken and even more so when the seven trumpets sound, so that the first and second "woes" are already proclaimed over it, the birth of the Messiah-child from the sun-woman must still be expected before the old dragon falls down upon the earth and the two blasphemous beasts join it from the sea and the land, so that the final "woe" is proclaimed that resounds to the end. This hellish trinity can appear only after the Word of God has become flesh and the sevenfold Holy Spirit has been poured out over the world. For as the Son who becomes flesh proceeds from the divine Father, so the first beast is the product of the dragon and the blasphemy of the Incarnation of God (for this reason, the great whore sits on it); and as the Spirit interprets the truth of the love between Father and Son, so the second beast with "two horns like a lamb and [that] spoke like a dragon", the spirit of lies who works false miracles, the spirit of ideology and propaganda, opposes the Holy Spirit. In the service of the anti-incarnation, he seduces the world so that it causes all, "both small and great, both rich and poor, both free and slave, to be marked on the right hand or the forehead, so that no one can buy or sell unless he has the mark, that is, the name of the beast or the number of its name" (Rev 13:16–17).

Atheism in the true sense, as antitheism, has been in existence only since after Christ. The materialism of Democritus or Lucretius was something completely different, a sort of tragic piety. In the post-Christian era, atheism in its most consistent form is the postulate that man, in order not to be alienated anymore but to attain "positive humanism", must not owe his existence to anybody except himself: this is the goal to which the whole economic and cultural process of the world must steer. The ideologies that are most powerful in the world today, whether they were proposed by Feuerbach or Marx or Nietzsche or Freud, meet in this demand. Christianity cannot avoid confrontation with it. All other attempts at escape (for example, Eastern meditation, which is practically dead in the East and not genuinely repeatable in the West) cannot evade the rule of the antitrinity. There may be many sectlike splinter religions that emerge and are soon submerged. The fight of that three-headed power is not against them but against the "called, elect, and faithful" who ride to battle together with the Lamb, the children of the sunwoman who "keep the commandments of God and the faith of Jesus".

The time of the "Enlightenment", which some theologians still want to bring to its end, truly ended long ago. *Aggiornamento* does not mean assimilating oneself to the atheist Enlightenment (to the point of declaring the autonomy of human conscience); instead, it means being abreast of the times in order to give that Enlightenment an authentic response.

The situation of the Christian is similar to a war on two fronts. On the one hand, he must fight along with all those who seek to keep the earth, God's creation, pure and holy against the diabolical spiritual and material destruction; on the other hand, by this action of making the earth subject according to God's will and of humanizing it, he unexpectedly lands in the group of those who are unfaithful to God under the pretext of being faithful to the earth. Christians are experiencing, as no generation before, how ambiguous all earthly progress is, how easily and almost automatically the instruments that give man power over time and space put him suddenly into chains and dehumanize him. And the more material power falls to him, the more the blocks of power concentrate themselves—necessarily against each other. For material power drifts of itself toward the spirit that is against God and toward the increased will to power. It would be an unimaginable paradox if humanity knew how to administer and distribute the fullness of power given to it in the Spirit of the One who came, not to rule, but to serve.

One cannot deny that it is more difficult today to be objectively a Christian than it was in earlier times. There is no longer any shelter. One can neither take refuge in progressive society, mistrusting the Church, nor snuggle into the Church in traditionalist fashion to hide from the demands of society. The heart of the Church herself is laid bare and even pierced like that of her Lord, so that anyone who wishes to take shelter in her enters into something naked and wounded. The monstrance in which the Host is exposed is itself exposed, and the Christian must decide to be so with it and in it. And the monstrance, the Church, exposed together with her Lord, becomes as insignificant as he: "no form or comeliness that we should look at him" (Is 53:2). But then why must everyone still "see him, every one who pierced him" (Rev 1:7)? Why is there still in this formless being the epitome of all form that draws all eyes to itself in fascination?

The solution for the Christian is clear: neither magical formulas with which one wishes to impress the form of Christ upon the world nor swearing by forms that life has left behind can bring salvation. The only thing that brings salvation is concentration

upon the one form that is at the same time unequivocal and eucharistically all-embracing, the only one
that is wide open to the infinite, to triune divine
love, and just as open to creation, since everything
exists for the sake of that form and has its stabil-
ity in it, everything that through it is to be sheltered in absolute love. Only this form—and thus
the end returns to the beginning—is finally the
incomparable.

POSTSCRIPT

Only a few catchwords have found room in this primer and only those that concern the faith of the Church and its interpretation and realization today. Many other aspects are not discussed, but some of them can become clearer by a sufficiently careful consideration of what has been said and also by relating the individual chapters to each other.

What was not dealt with are all questions concerning the ethical discipline of the Church, even though they appear most urgent for the faithful—laymen as well as clerics. Questions of laymen: contraception, abortion, premarital sex; questions of the clergy: celibacy as obligatory for priests; questions of religious: meaning and relevance of the evangelical counsels today. The priesthood of women was briefly dealt with in the chapter "Mary–Church–Office".

To be given the proper response, the ethical questions call for another primer. Two thoughts must suffice here. The first was hinted at in the chapter "Reinterpreting": problems of Church discipline—in contrast to dogmatic truths—are to a certain extent variable, subjected to the judgment of the Church, which examines them anew in each epoch in the light of the Gospel. Everybody knows that a "disengagement" of priesthood and celibacy is in principle possible. The great question is whether it is opportune for the spiritual good of the Church and whether those who demand it so persistently are considering this spiritual good. Analogous points hold for the questions of the sexual sphere.

This brings us to the second thought. Christians differ greatly in how close or far they stand from the radiant, glowing core of the Gospel. There are innumerable gradations. Ecclesial law, however, cannot have regard for these gradations. It has its precise formulation, which must not aim at a tepid average but must remain as close to the Gospel as possible. Only the interpretation can show generosity and mercy in regarding human weakness, according to the principle called *epieikeia* [equity] by the law of the Eastern Church. But in formulating her discipline, the Church of Christ cannot listen to the protests and demands of a multitude that is influenced by the spirit of the times or manipulated by clever leaders. (Collecting ever so many signatures—something that is easily organized—does not prove or move anything.) To the great multitude it will always seem impossible and even inhuman to follow Christ. Nevertheless, the Church seeks to look at her children with the eyes of Christ and judges accordingly what she thinks she must demand from them. She will hear and consider complaints that are made in the spirit of Christ.

Further: most admit that the sense for what the New Testament calls "sin" has melted away except for a few remains. The almost complete disappearance of the sacrament of confession attests to it. In earlier times, perhaps, the consciousness of sin was not always in the central place where it should have been, namely, in the lack of love of God and neighbor. But when someone considers this center, how can he think he is without sin—perhaps grievous sin? One trembles when one sees whole parishes streaming up to receive the Host without confession and often probably without repentance. Do they discern the Body of the Lord, as Paul demands, and do they not eat their own judgment? One must pray this does not happen.

But perhaps the faithful are not sufficiently taught reverence for the (literally!) Holy of Holies, not even the difference between sacred and profane, between the world and God's Presence in it. "Do you not know that you are members of Christ?" Paul asks. Perhaps they really do not know it because nobody tells them.

It is impossible to prevent the disintegration of ethics in a society that cannot live within a comprehensive natural law anymore as the *polis* of antiquity did (because nature has been turned into mere material for technology), a society that has also used up the remains of Christian ethics to the point of debating whether there still are "basic values". One cannot hope that the situation will regulate itself. The only genuine hope lies in a Christianity that lets itself be confronted anew with its incomparable origin and with the glory, the radiant grace, and the equally radiant demands of that origin. The maxim of action, of *ethos*, always needs a *logos* that precedes it and gives it its meaning. In Christ, the eternal *Logos*, God's Word of meaning for the world and for mankind, has come among us bodily. By giving full meaning to human existence, he has also given the true maxim of human action; he lived this maxim; even more, he has proved identical with it. One merely has to look at this "light of the world" that has shown itself to us unobscured by any cloud. "And men loved darkness rather than light"; every one did not wish "to come to the light, lest his deeds should be exposed" (Jn 3:19f.). Some cover themselves with the clouds of atheism, others in those of a Christian skepticism, which protects itself from the naked light by means of various anthropological filters like billows of fog.

Thus the man is sought who "is sent from God ... for testimony, to bear witness to the light, that all might believe through him. He was not the light, but came to bear witness to the light. The true light that enlightens every man was coming into the world. He was in the world ..." (Jn 1:7–9).